Nocturnal Omissions
A Tale of Two Poets

poems by Gavin Geoffrey Dillard
and Eric Norris

SiblingRivalryPress
www.siblingrivalrypress.com

Nocturnal Omissions: A Tale of Two Poets.

Sibling Rivalry Press, LLC
13913 Magnolia Glen Drive
Alexander, AR 72002

www.siblingrivalrypress.com

Library of Congress Control Number: 2011933009

ISBN: 978-1-937420-00-0

First Sibling Rivalry Press Edition, September 2011

❧

Acknowledgements

Gavin and Eric would like to thank Bryan Borland, Scott Dillard, Michael Lassell, Patrizio Santoro, and Ian Young for their involvement in this book. Some of Eric's poems here have been published in *The Nervous Breakdown* and *Softblow;* some of Gavin's poems have been published in *Chiron Review*.

Contents

❦

How to Write a Foreword for a Book of Poems
For Dionysus and his maenads, Eric and Gav

First, know a poet for 40 years, since he was still a teenager and you
were not.

Think: That was many hairs ago, white hairs—head, face, and chest.

Then be minding your business one afternoon and violate all
rules of the hermit's hut by opening an e-mail that makes the request.

Think: "Fuck! How do I get out of this without hurting anyone's
feelings?"
Say, on the other hand, "Of course."

Mean them both.
After all, toleration of ambivalence is a sign of maturity.
Like arthritis.

Receive the manuscript like a good electronic-age scribbler.
Think: This file is not as slim a volume as most.

You have never heard of poet number two, never read him.
He means nothing to you except through the vessel of Gavin.

Google the acolyte/apprentice/disciple/devotee—
what's a website for?

Remember Gavin in L.A. wearing little more than his boa constrictor, his
photo of you in San Francisco, your photo of him in a garden.
How Timothy Leary screamed like an enraged jackal
at the chair he broke at Gavin's party a few glitter-and-eyeliner
decades before the wild child became Rilke to a younger man.

Read the poems.

Read them with your browser open because there are no footnotes.

Wonder why you don't happen to speak Latin or even Italian or
know the names of the deities of the world's major religions
or have any clue who Zachary Quinto may be
or the botanical names
for things these word boys like to plant in the soil when not planning to
plant themselves in each other.

Be amazed at the samurai edge between reality and fantasy,
between poetry and the countless things that are not
poetry, and the willingness
to dive into a
rapture of words, to tear the sheets of them, with a stranger.

To hook up syntactically before anything else.

Wonder how Gavin learned so much since Paul Roche's poetry class
at CalArts all those white hairs ago when his were long and dark and
yours were light and short and both were silky
with potential,
anticipation,
aspiration.
Goating around the universe for half a century appears to be
instructive.

Wonder what you could possibly say about the poems that the poems
do not say for themselves.

Wonder what you should say to the reader before their reading begins.

Think: This is the record of a passion.

Think: This is the record of a passion between two men (the universal is
in the particular; Be Specific, as Strunk & White say).

Nocturnal Omissions, you see, is the story in verse of the
great passion of an elder for a younger man—
or did old Oscar use the word *affection* for his affliction,
keeping passion at arm's length?

Nocturnal Omissions is the story of double passions, like the twin helixes of DNA,
of hunger for
expression and spirit as rubicund, lubricious as a ripened pomegranate.

If the Apollonian and Dionysian of Nietzsche's model are authentic antitheses,
then the synthesis is as true for comedy as it is for tragedy, as these poems attest: Every true comedy ends in a marriage.

Wonder who will be shocked by the poems and who will only
pretend to be shocked.
Remember your basic Noël Coward: "It's discouraging how many people are shocked by honesty and how few by deceit."

Note that these Ping-Ponging poems have a large, impressive supporting cast:
Hadrian and Antinous,
Verlaine and Rimbaud,
Siva and Krisna,
David and Jonathan,
Emily and Edna.

More names: Ovid, Blake, Priapus, and James McAvoy;
Gyllenhaal (Jake), Gandalf, and Shakespeare's Gloucester;
Rumi, Hafiz, Mirabai, Mishima;
Anderson Cooper, Diane Arbus, Ewan McGregor,
and God, of course, implicit and ex, singular and plural,
upper case and pagan lower.

Note that poignancy and longing and separation and loss and mortality
are part of this universe, too.

But what is passion?

More than the name of a perfume or fruit:
It has as many aspects as a fly's eye and many fluids,
multiple xylem and phloem.

Many accents and means of dictation.

Duly note for the reader, dear reader, that some *Nocturnal* inflections are French and Greek (in both the semantic and catamitic senses) and involve vases and Romantic poets of the past.

Some of the words, however, will be specified of necessity in better commercial dictionaries as "vulgar"—four-letter symbols for feelings that refuse etymology.

Think of the words your brain conjures when their words hit: courtship, courtesan, coy voyeur, mortal voyager, internet Bacchanal, mythic, mimesis, messianic, and masturbation.

Remember that the vulgate is the language of the people.

These poets would rather be pineapples than professors.

Be surprised at how playful this serial poetry is, how fast and spontaneous, though certainly not without discipline in both the formulaic and pornographic meanings of the word—Apollonian *and* Dionysian.

Amuse yourself while enjoying the rhymes and unrhymes, the allusions and allures and the simultaneous seductions of two who have already committed themselves to consummation devoutly to be wished.

Think again: What can be said?

Write: Sex and poetry and spiritual enlightenment are the triplet appetites in this ravenous anti-world of Eric and Gavin as they grapple toward Bethlehem or Nirvana, or a farm in North Carolina, a beach on Maui, an East Village side street, a mountaintop near a sacred city in Japan.

Maybe love is the fourth horseman of this apotheosis— or perhaps "whoresman" would be better. Or not.

Realize that there is no reason a god should not grovel with a god, a goat,
or a goddess,
no earthly or celestial reason a mere mortal should not aspire to ascension.
Perhaps the term should be "mere divinity."

Perhaps there are no divisions, no dichotomies.

Perhaps love and sex and passion and poetry are not bipolar.

Note that there are 111 poems in this free exchange
of secrets and secretions, a magical, mystical number,
an arithmetic angel pin-dancing with the pan-flute god.

Remember that getting on a ship or a plane is not the only way to
take a journey.
A book can be the circumnavigation of a galaxy
(ask Kirk and Spock).

Nocturnal Omissions is an epistolary diary in verse of two beings who meet
when their spiritual paths inadvertently cross in the woods on a
snowy/jasmine-scented evening, six thousand miles apart. The poems are
naked but not nude. They bare all and bear close scrutiny. They are full of
fun and truth and passion of all kinds, from the erotic to the
metaphysical. They are shocking and comforting, sacred and profanely
profound.

    Michael Lassell
    New York City

❦

Prologue

In the summer of twenty-ten I met a young lad on Facebook named Eric Norris. He was a poet and had responded to some comment about one of my books, *A Day for a Lay*. Eric was cute, of course, seemed to regard my work highly, and so I introduced myself.

I lived on Maui at the time, and Eric in the Big Grapple. With a click we became "friends" and began chatting. It was a matter of a day or two before he sent me a poem. I responded in kind, Eric retaliated, and so it began. We wrote every day.

Merely a handful of poems into this, and I suggested the possibility of a book. Eric agreed immediately, and Bryan Borland of Sibling Rivalry Press, who had been watching our play, agreed immediately to publish the thing. Our working title was *The Courtship of Passion*.

Now, I was slated to, six weeks down the road or so, read at the big NCA media conference in San Francisco. I was the featured author within the gay contingent, and a couple of scholars were doing presentations about me as "The Naked Poet"—a moniker once bestowed by the LA Times. Given the theme, then, it seemed essential that I once again read in-the-buff.

I am in my fifties—tho remain reasonably fit—and it has been years since I've exposed my wobbly bits to the literati. So I figured it might be nice to have some fresh wobblies to back me up, and so asked Eric—who immediately agreed. And thus the presence of a publisher and the eventuality of a fixed meet-up became themes within the "letters."

One other thing I want to mention is that we also kept up a practically air-tight vigil of emails. We sent hundreds. We had discussed including portions of our mailings as a part of the collection, as certain points in certain poems allude to themes, photographs, even video exchanged in cyberspace.

But there is only so much a book can do. In the end, we thought it best to trust the imagination of the reader and let the poetry speak for itself. We hope that you'll agree.

In joy!
Gavin Dillard
Black Mountain, NC

❦ 17 ❦

Nocturnal Omissions
A Tale of Two Poets

La Fin des Temps

It is now the End of Days—why mince parables or
morality? all that we have will be lost,
 all that we are shall be found;
have I made myself perfectly clear? have I wrestled your
 heart from its stronghold of thorns and
trampled that horny copse with my befevered hooves?
 Let me be frank: time is short, and before the
spacepeople come with their mighty galactic ways, and
 Jesus arrives to *tsch-tsch* our ineptitudes ...
before the tides have abolished coastal cities and the
 nether-sections swept up in vast cacophonies of
devil winds ...
 before the Ark sets afloat and the Tardis
touches down ...
 I want to supplant your blood with my sperm and
plant a garden of teeth upon island and crest;
 I want to consume all your rivers and plunder dank
forests.
 Until all that has been found be lost again,
and where we end
 is the beginning of something Terrible and Profound.

The Day of Apocalypse

It's hard to see my future as a land
rising from magma deposits, orange
rivers of lava, pyroclastic clouds,
volcanic vomitus boiling from blue
waves. I must have some sort of blind spot.

I creep forward like the Earl of Gloucester
in *King Lear*, smelling my way to Dover.
I shower. When I pull a washcloth between
my legs, after my morning dump, things
in Dover can look pretty bad. I hang

the soiled cloth on a steel rail to dry,
then I soap up my hands. I pluck my peach
cleft aside, rinsing off an asterisk—
the Southern star I have so often used
to orient myself at night, sliding

through the sea in search of spices. I
survey my world through a tiny vent,
a window cracked to let the steam escape.
I can see Queens: a tall oak tree, and three
old ladies with Ziplocs full of cooked rice.

The Fates! A Buddhist with a bowl accepts
their offerings with a bow of thanks.
I'm thankful, too—for what I can perceive:
green leaves and gratitude. Tomorrow might
erupt like a volcano, I suppose,

blowing me sky-high. I'll cope. Maybe
I will land in your arms, if it does.

Petit Déjeuner au Lit

Tonight I made a lovely, creamy garlic and white
asparagus bisque: I browned my garlic, onion, parsnip,
 asparagus and a potato, puréed them with cream and beaucoup
butter, added salt and pepper, a dash of cayenne, and finally
 stirred in a flood of fresh goat milk;
it was heaven, darling, and I wish you could have
 partaken.

Perhaps "landscape" is too grandiose a term: I'm thinking more
diminutive and immediate—a garden—my own personal row of
Phaseolus vulgaris;
let's take for instance the puckered corolla of your sphincter,
 if I plant my seed in that fecund bunching, how long before it will
bear me fruit, how rich the harvest, and for how long do you
 suppose it might feed me?

Not that I am not happy with soup, you understand: I am a
simple monk making my way up the Mountain, I do not
 require large quantities of meat, nor are sweets and superfluities of
indulgence of any particular interest.
 But a proper Brussels sprout or roasted yam can make my
heart skip a pace, the nectar of a ripe Georgia peach percolating
 through the hairs of my chest is cause for braying;

if I kiss your face half the night and sleep the rest with a
thigh wedged against your groin, will I awake to breakfast-in-
 bed: will a hot stream of piss be mine and a fleshy scone of
rubicund jam? may I sink my teeth into the roan nape of your
 neck and relish the savory spice of your pain?
You bring out the chef in me; I want to
 eat you by the spoonful, wear the peelings like brocade ....

Crossing Legs

Help me hold it. If I wake tonight,
will you place your thigh against my crotch?
I'll pillow you in pubic hair so light,
so curly and so warm. Let me watch

your silver chest descending as you sleep,
illuminated by a square of moon.
Shift your weight slightly, should I creep
up with an erection. It's too soon.

Move again and bring your leg to rest
a little higher. Close to tears, un-
able to dissolve, I will confess—
I've got to go, to piss, I'm dying. None

could endure such torture. "Hold it in,
babe. This is love," whisper with your shin.

Out of the Fire, Into the Pan

I like that you're smarter than me,
I like that you're naïver than me;
 I don't mind that you're younger than me (though I have
traditionally preferred older dudes);
 I love that we haven't met and yet
feel so deeply as though we had.

 I like that you're shorter than me (not that there's
anything wrong with tall—but I can imagine bouncing
 you upon my lap like a tittering tot),
I love that you've loved in seven languages (for I have
 so many yet to go);
I love that you have yet to find "home" (so that
 I can offer you mine).

 I am an old goat enjoying my pasture; you are a kid on the
streets of uncertainty:
 I fall into the tradition of such ancient beasts as Dionysius and
Aegipan, Cernunnos and Siva, hornéd gods of
 forest and field;
you a wandering pixie of a delusional dell.

 It may take time to get used to your shrill laugh (which
sounds more cathartic than ecstatic—still riddled with
 childhood's unreckoned angst); it will
take no time getting used to your hot, moist colon, which
 even across six thousand miles of ocean and
desert, fits me like a
         kid glove.

To My Muse

Let me taste your taste,
my arms about your waist:
empty every drop
into my mouth. Don't stop.

A Midsummer Night's Doggerel

Fluids have I plenty, my son,
temperance have I none;
never tease a horny bard with
metaphors unspun!

The Dance of Shiva

Before this world was formed, I played a role
hitherto reserved only for darkness:
I was the void in which you poured your soul.

I am the first, the last, the beautiful
Truth—Keats's amphora—I shall outlast
all other vessels. Nothing, that's my role

in the great cosmic drama. I'm the whole
of time itself set spinning by your presence.
I was the void in which you poured your soul

so long ago—before a god could hold
a paltry thing like man and love him as
his equal. Let's give warmth a larger role

in this new universe. Space was so cold,
so lifeless, dark and empty in the past.
I was the void in which you poured your soul—

the mouth, the Milky Way, the gloryhole—
ten thousand other gods have used. But that's
the past. I am nothing again: my role
tonight is infinite. Come fill my soul.

Suicide for 2

I have two nooses, one for
you and one for me. Let's die to
 this life and be born again, together
on a farm somewhere, where
 time is snail-paced and two dusty lads may
share a bed. Let's quiver and
 giggle during thunderstorms and
gawk dumbfounded at endless
 skies full of endless stars.

Let us make this easy: long before the
years of puberty shall we share
 blood from self-inflicted
wounds, bury teeth we have lost within the
 trunk of a tree that bears our knife-
etched names; we'll mix our spittles together in
 dirty palms and smear it across our
foreheads before plunging to our
 certain deaths from the branches of
trees above lazy rivers filled with
 mythical beasts.

I can read your scars like a bible, for
half of them I inflicted myself, the
 others I watched you perform with
Cherokee war-whoops and machines that
 ought to have flown; I have seen you
naked running willy-nilly through the
 poplars and smelled with lustful glee the
nasty thumbs that we pressed into each
 other's groins.

Let us die now together from our
lands so far apart, where sirens
 shriek, where soulless politicians wave and
rant and preachers vomit vitriol about
 anyone who doesn't eat the same pathetic
breakfast cereal; let us meet together in a
 land ruled by hobbits, dwarves and
dinosaurs in flannel vests ...

I have two nooses, both weaved from
letters and poems received and sent.
 They contain your dreams, your faith, your
scent; I share one with you, my poet my
 friend, with the queries: What is life, if
but the brutal matrix of
 aloneness; and
What is Love, if not worth
 dying for?

Simple Gifts

Of all the nooses I have chosen—ties,
nylon laundry line, black leather belts,
fairy hands fumbling at my throat—I
found none completely equal to the task
of enhancing my orgasms—and what's worse,

un-poetic in the extreme. Always,
I wound up bug-eyed, twitching, coughing my-
self silly, dildo dislodged, coins of cum
scattered all across my hardwood floors,
dissolving the polyurethane finish.

I have no desire to wake up in Heaven
hanging from a big brass doorknob like
a retired Tory politician—even
a member of Mrs. Thatcher's cabinet.
Mom would never forgive me. So, I am

glad to have you here, thinking ahead.
Let us die a nice American death,
clean and simple as a Shaker hymn:
on hands and knees, your arm around my neck,
our eyes upturned in prayer, cock in ass.

We Are that We Are

Funny thing about God: people mistake God for some
callous, cold fuck. Where did *that* come from?

Certainly not the Old Testament dude with his pre- and
post-marital mismatches, his obsession with stones and
semen and strings of foreskin like cranberries on a
Mithramas tree; hell, even the word "testament" is
derived from the word "testes."

Rumi and Hafiz wooed Allah like Jonathan hounded
David, and Siva of course was running through the
woods in a pair of horns before Cernunnos or Pan had
munched their first leaves of ivy or downed their
first jug of Chianti.

The fact of the matter is that God is both the
manifest *and* the unmanifest—flesh and spirit, as
Jesus attests—and that blood and sperm, sweat and
piss, are the oils that grease the wheels of
creation;

and that you, dear supplicant, have made
offerings, which, burnt and unburnt, pleaseth me
greatly, and I intend to multiply your offspring like the
fishes of the sea,
        … or, well, kill us both trying.

Daedalus and Icarus

Behold my blue bath towel: a
clean place to masturbate. My fate
falls to its surface, like wax
and feathers. There is no escape

for me. I'm Icarus tonight,
delighting in that dizzy dash
upward—ever upward—toward
a small, heart-breaking splash

below. Watch as my white hand
disappears in the Aegean.

To Eric on his Birthday

Happy birthday Happy birthday, my
cranky Calliope, may the gods bless you with
absolution and bestow upon thee multitudinous
sins worthy of absolving. (Were I there I could
guarantee your soul's-worth ....)

Were I there I would raise the parental eye-
brows of Mnemosyne and Zeus, making
waves with their most lustrous darling until
even Uncle Poseidon peers over the brow of our
flailing papyrela;

so let me toast you from afar, my ever-
turgid muse, a Hendrick's-and-Pellegrino with a
lime partly sucked, a drunken paramour in his
far-away garden beneath a full full moon, and the
blendings of jasmine and pits ripe from an

afternoon at the gym. You are loved and
treasured in my most private places, yearned for and
lusted over as the summer's first peach, from my
gonads, my soul, and on the breath of my
speech: Happy birthday, young man—here at least
remains a candle unblown.

To My Teacher

Sitting on the toilet,
reading one of your poems,
a speck of something
slowly moving
catches my eye.

A spider seems to be
spinning a web between
the ivory ribs
of my asthmatic radiator—
exactly at the height

a heart beat when
I was a boy.

In the past,
I might have seized
the toilet brush beside me—
killed the creature instantly—
with childish glee.

Now, I continue
reading, enjoying my shit,
peeing with pleasure,
turning to another
beautiful poem.

It is my birthday.
Thanks for the present.

Epiphany

Aloha young sir,
the poem was from me,
 the spider from God;

 indeed, I am pleased to be a
part of your toilette. I can
 think of but one better position to
have your fixed and
 undivided attention;

 for now, I will take that
precious moment when the
 sphincter is engaged and the
mind on hold, for such is
 meditation and I could never

scold you for being of a
 silent mien, with the
grunt and the sigh which must
 surely follow—Epi-
phany, as it were. Your

 hollow places are sacred—to
me and to God—I hope to
 make them my home.

A Stick of Incense

The litter other lovers
leave always appears
so poignant in the dark:
Kleenex, condoms, sad
old ghosts, exchanging
ectoplasmic spasms.

Let us leave nothing
sad as this behind—
not even our footprints—
just our scent, the smell of
something burning
sweetly. Let us leave

one stick of incense, so
wherever we may go
we go together, hand
in hand—aware
that, fuck or suck, we
knelt on holy ground.

Giridhara

Mon amant, I fear you mistake us: this
is no ordinary tryst, no pathetic
 Verlaine awaiting his brat lover, no
Izumi Shikibu yearning for that
 wanton prince; oh no,

 we are Mirabai awaiting the
presence of her Dark Lord, and when He
 comes the world will quake the heavens
thunder and the very gods sink profoundly into
 humblest reverie;

 and when that Terrible Presence has
passed, when the evening of our
 concupiscence has been requited and
the warbles of morning have
 begun their perfunctory praises:

 shall we find naught but ashes, scratched
upon our chest and head, which then we
 shall wear boldly into the Sunlight, the
children of shadows no more:

Om Kleem Krisnaya Namah!

Emily and Edna

Were I Emily Dickinson, as well I
might have been (between the Ménière's Disease and my
 new-found virginity) and were you
Edna St Vincent Millay (who, after all, developed a
 reputation as a bit of a slut), I would invite your
ink-stained hands inside my womb, in the
 throes of feminine camaraderie, with pen and
pad, to write of all you find
 there;

were I Emily (as I had been William Blake, and
Ono no Komachi before him), I would
 scribble from my sick bed that we
both became enlightened, you in your
 Renascence meadow surrounded by the mountains of
Truth, me from the fragilest of creatures that made
 residence in our tiny Amherst garden;
and that together we shook the world, dearest
 friend, sui generis,

and slew the beasts of prosaic mediocrity.

Edna Sends a Letter from Kyoto

I must apologize for the delay
in writing this. The flight from
New York was Hell—
cramped, full of crying, food
inedible. Still, you get hungry and
you eat, and you receive
constipation for
your pains. I'm never flying
coach again. But here

I am, Emily—Japan!
My hotel, the Garden Palace, has
put me in a cherry blossom
room—all pink—synthetic
silk bedspread, rice paper sheets.
The usual Hokusai reprint
leans from the wall above my bed
ready to drown my dreams:
'The Great Wave
off Kanagawa.' You've seen it.
Mount Fuji, little boat,
dark tsunami looming
over it with foamy fingers.
You might think the people of
Japan only produced
one great picture.

You asked about the temples.
Well, they're gigantic,
old and everywhere.
They all sell amulets and prayers—
long life, fertility, good fortune—
the standard wishes.
I bought all three for you,

dear, and one more
which shall, for now,
remain a mystery.

I rang their bells, smelled
their smells, found too many
monks attractive. Their grounds
overwhelm the senses
with such tightly controlled
forms of beauty: thick bamboo
groves, curious flowers,
a million varieties of moss.
They are about as close
to Heaven you can get
without jumping off
a cliff, I think. If only
the water in the ponds didn't
seem so still, in certain places,
so serene, so stagnant,
such big brown eyes of
unfulfilled desires.
I would only consider
living here in a
missionary capacity.

You asked about the Ryoan-ji
temple specifically,
that famous rock garden.
This puzzled me
at first—the whole idea of
planting rocks outside
cemeteries. I had a look
for you today.
This is what I saw:
14 boulders, older
than anything built by
man. They sit on grass
medallions, surrounded by
combed white gravel. The brochure
says there are 15 boulders, but

from any seated angle just
14 are visible. Enlightenment
occurs when you can see
15, rise above
terrestrial concerns—
position, time and place—
I sat there for 2 hours
seeing 14 and I left
mildly frustrated.

Frustrated, that is, until
I wrote the word
'frustrated,' for you,
Emily, up there. Then I saw
my 15th boulder, yes, just then.
The word 'frustrated' put
the whole thing in
a Zen perspective: it is love.
Love is the one concern
I do find difficult
to rise above…

Metaphorically Yours

Dearest Woman-of-the-Peafowl—oh, no,
that was Carson—well, whatever; Dearest
 Madame Bard, you have my heart and my
unwavering pen, my lust and my
 curiosity: of what bizarre sea creatures have you
eaten today? are a geisha's hands as soft as they
 say?

From my Massachusetts retreat I can only
imagine your enthrall at that magnificent
 mountain, rising above Kyoto like a great,
snowy-nippled breast; have you onsened yet with the
 Macaca fuscata? Are they ominous, and
do they have the decency to remove themselves to
 defecate?

I miss you. I want you. Could I regain my
equilibrium, I would fly to where you are (a
 curious notion for a grounded sparrow such as
myself); were this bed not binding me, I would
 utilize its linen wrappings to entrap you against
my side. But don't
 mistake,

'tis not that I'm suggesting anything as
prosaic and plebian as marriage. No, just because
 poets should have the right to
marry, does not mean that they should
 exercise that right—any more than that men
should amble off to war (unless of course one finds the
 blood of handsome young men poetic, but that is
subject for quite another poem, n'est-çe
 pas?). What I mean to say is

the bumble bees in my petite garden hum
madly in your absence, but it is of
little console for a dying virgin in a
distant century. Bring me tiding soon, man to
man, metaphor to metaphor;

let us tie our foreskins into a knot and be
done with this confounded brooding!

Dolly

You hardly even know me.
Before we tie our bowels in
knots, answer me this:

Who is the juvenile
delinquent up above?
Clearly a tough customer—
as one can tell—
bald head, bully-boy bill,
black, surgical stitching
around her neck—
something stolen from
Frankenstein's lab.

It must have been bad—
quite a fracas.

It looks as if they tried
to pull her head off,
peer inside, and
they, whoever they may be,

nearly succeeded. How this act
affected her judgment, her subsequent
attitudes on Art or Life,
spectators can
only speculate.

Still, there is something
there, a ghost, perhaps,
a zigzag clue,
that crude stitching—a
homemade, almost
child-like quality—which
suggests to our
psychologist, Dr. Boyd,
this unusual creature
was not a stranger
to tenderness—to what,
in a simpler time,
we might have
understood as—love.

Her whereabouts
are presently unknown—
probably a dresser drawer
somewhere, dreaming
under the underwear.

Her mother, Diane,
our forensic photographer,
fears Dolly is dead
and is herself hysterical,
hardly able to speak.
She had to be
sedated. Sad.

Finally, ladies and gentle-
men, before we go
knocking on doors with her photo,
disturbing the dead,
I would like to

circulate a description of Dolly
supplied by her step-
brother, Geoffrey,
a good, reliable man,
a local veterinarian.
His portrait may be
some use to us.

Good luck.

Her mouth reminds me of a platypus—
A duck—the last of the wild red mallards. Sure,
She might be stuffed like any one of us,
But could you survive a suit of raw velour?

Her origins are wrapped in mystery.
The tag stitched to one stump still reads, "Korea."
One wonders—North or South? The DMZ?
Dolly does not discuss her past. I fear,

Nothing—noise—not even naphthalene—
Has prevented moths nibbling holes in her back.
(Moths, which I should add, I've never seen—
Except as powder, palpable as ash.)

A photo of the two of us exists
Somewhere. We look much smaller. She's the one
Appearing to examine the goldfish
Swimming around their cool, ceramic sun.

An Aperture Monograph

Today I am Diane Arbus, fotographing the man with
two penises, the one that rises across the fur of your
 belly, and the other that I keep tucked inside my
left lung—that obstructs my breath, but throbs ever
 so near my heart,

 reminding me that death and life are inextricably
interwoven; I have tattooed your name inside my
 left thigh (no, not *"Rosebud,"* the other name ...) and
when I pump down there I imagine more than
 just the ink contorting with each tensile

 thrust; when I pull up pictures of you I am Burt
Lancaster straddling the mast of a sailing vessel shrieking
 "I'm a happy bird!!!" ... but when I truly think of
you I realize that I don't have a clue who you really
 are—do you smoke, do

 you drink to excess, do you show kindness to
strangers? when I am sick will you nurse me with
 joy; when you are sick will you allow yourself to be
coddled? are you good with the non-theoreticals? is
 there blood behind your honéd words?

 Diane would know, but she is
dead, and now everything has gone
 digital; the freak show has begun, you've
paid your nickel, but do you really
 want to see?

Curriculum Vitae

Something human I can hold. If only
cameras captured living things. It seems like
we're coming to that freakish place where
men are less mythic, monolithic, flesh
and blood. This must be where the talk-
ing stops, we start to smell something strange,
like gas. We look into each other's eyes
and see our limits and desires for the first
time. "Is that the moon in there or me?"
We ask the odd homunculi reflected in
our skulls if these small images are souls,

our words wide open windows where
the breeze is soft and tropical. Or gas.
I'm in New York and I have nothing but
a leaky oven here to keep me warm—
words and pictures to manipulate:
the lease I signed allows no other pets.
Maybe I'll make a cup of tea. First
a piss. It sounds like rain. Listen. Words.
They have no taste, no texture, and no smell.
These are my poems. They are sad—pale
yellow substitutes for the pink tongue

I crave to run along your clean crack.
I wish that words were more reassuring
like maps. I've been studying your woods,
you know, North Carolina, your intended
home. I would kill to climb a tree. Should I
apply for a position there? A pine cone?
A cat? A forest pixie? I'll submit
a sample of my urine—my Curriculum
Vitae. Not my life. A sketch. A crude
outline in a tiddle-cup. Feel free
to test it, once you've fed the chickens.

My family is ... they're far away. I called
my granny twice a day for 20 years.
She had a massive stroke last summer, died
in church, just as I said the day before.
I never miss appointments. I'd prefer
a fling with Figaro to Madame Butterfly—
one happy ending to three hours of drama.
My favorite English poem is "To His
Coy Mistress." My favorite poet must be this
guy, Gavin Dillard, although it is a photo-
finish: you and Shakespeare tied with Ovid.

My cock is 19 inches. Hard. It is.
I've never measured its circumference, nor
received complaints about its size—just groans—
which don't count as complaints. I do like dogs.
I detest Mark Doty. Overwritten. Overrated.
I love one man at a time. I have this
trouble separating my dick from my heart.
I manage desolation with a dildo, since
it doesn't leave an aftertaste like bad cologne.
I'd rather swim than dance, unless it is
to slam with skins. I worry I will die alone.

Virtually Yours

Aloha, Sweetness. Ms Arbus thanks you for your responses and
so do I. I would have responded sooner, but the chickens have been in a
terrible ruckus all morning. Such testy little creatures; whether you
give them what they want or what they don't want they will
fuss at you nonetheless—rather like a great many poets we both may
        know …

But to the business at hand, as it were: I am more than aware that
we are dancing on a chimera of spider's silk—but is it ever the
truth that frightens us? Yes, the chemistry of journaling is vastly
different from that of jousting (Emily would know of the prior, tho
hardly of the latter …) but we can assume solace in the

knowledge that we will be left with our journal—much more than
most loves have bequeathed to me. And we can presume the san-
guinity that something of a lasting nature is being born (whether
crudely stitched or missing the occasional limb). And somehow I feel we
might find use for each other in bed—as long as our
        metaphors hold up!

As for the rudiments, I am 5'10" or 11", depending on the
evening preceding; I am anywhere between 6 and 8", depending on
who's measuring and the strength of my morning chai; your
pear simile was spot-on, as pear tarte tatin is my favorite
dessert; as for prowess, that is the least of my concerns—I am quite
certain we have digits and niches in plentitude to cover all our
        bases;

I abhor most pop music, tho would be willing to have either
Bono's and/or Carlos Marín's bambinos; Roberto Alagna could have
me for a single high note (and Ewa Podleś for a low note); I do have a
penchant for authentic folk and all genuine bluegrass (the Dillards are
indeed distant cousins); favorite films are *The Dead*, *Dear Frankie*, the
first ¾ of *Amarcord*, and anything starring James McAvoy; if I have a

favorite novel I cannot remember which (tho have read *Autobiography of a Yogi* more than any other tome); I

avoid contemporary poetry except when utterly obliged, and favorite poems would be any and every by Ono no Komachi—Lao Tzu and Mirabai rate highly as well. The rest is a matter of record in the Wikipedia, my memoir, and various other unverifiable sources; most important to our purposes is that I consider kissing more intimate than fucking, and entirely share your penchant for the male liqueur.

I regret only the loves that I've refused; my favorite color is moss-in-bloom; I'm more than a half-century old and have all the requisite nicks and dings; I have Ménière's disease and have to close my eyes frequently to reboot; I have no sexual preferences or restrictions—or, if I do, it is up to you to ferret them.

I am generous to a fault, if I had Anderson Cooper on a tether I would let you spank him first; I detest surprises—that trickster Oberon is neither friend nor associate; the dreary, clichéd, serial fags of San Francisco and New York make me gag;

I find homosexuals who shave their testicles repugnant, and I have never made it all the way thru a Lady Gaga tune—*there, I said it!*

So now I have bunnies to feed and the gym to attend—that I might be ripe for our first encounter (keep in mind, it's been a half decade for me, so *please* don't be gentle); know that I desire to be, in every way conceivably possible to man and spirit, that which reaches inside you and grasps you by the glands.

Your joy is my lust; your tears my treasure,
kisses where ya pisses,
Gav

Reading the Auspices

Yes, I am going to the Priest.
There's no point in concealing it.
I've lost two pounds. Nothing
feels at home inside my mouth.
I cannot eat. Strange prodigies
surround me. Just yesterday,

the clerical collar of a cock—
a very snug white foreskin
belonging to a beautiful Pole—
evaporated before my very eyes—
in a puff of satanic smoke—
when I opened the steamroom door.

If this were not bad enough—
I suffered an erection when
I was assaulted in Grand Central
by cinnamon and baked apples—
so strong a scent the station
took on Edenic overtones.

Tonight, I donned a sweaty black
pair of running shorts and ran
to my bodega for beer—into
a pair of trannies. They squeezed
my testicles so hard with their eyes
my balls began to bleed like stones.

Are these good signs or bad? Each day
I get a billet-doux—a poem.
Am I in love? I wonder. Will
the poems cease if my guts
run out of fresh entrails for you
to read, review, and analyze?

Ewa's Immortal Requiem

It was some years ago at Davies Symphony Hall in San
Francisco—Herbert Blomstedt conducting, I should
think—Verdi's *Requiem*. Some of my memory has become
vague; but of the gist I remain absolutely clear:

there were four vocalists, two men, two ladies; probably a
tenor and a baritone-bass—it does not matter—a soprano and
an alto. I (we) remember the alto: Ewa Podleś.

I cannot recall the order; it seems that the men had their
solos first, after which stepped up the soprano. She was a
large thing, bedecked in tinsel and glass—what we now call
bling. And she sang, quite beautifully, if grandly;

lastly (at least in my version) approached Ms Podleś. Not a
large woman (the soprano towered above her), dressed in a
simple black frock—for all secular purposes she would have
been construed as the soprano's handmaid; and then

something happened—and I cannot tell the tale without
weeping and trembling all over!—Ms Podleś opened her
mouth and a note came out that—*how can one speak of
such a thing?*—that shook the fabric of creation;

it was *the* Perfect Note: Ms Podleś touched God.

With today's digital imagery one might imagine such a
scene from *Star Trek* or *Doctor Who*—a force came out of
the alto's depths that proceeded to ripple through the
front row, second row, and out across the theatre; I

caught it in the front row of the loge, where I had the
privilege of watching the wave's effect on the entire
audience. Ms Podleś continued singing, but no one was

the same after or since—people stared transfixed, some

whispered excitedly, many lost in meditation; years
later I conferred with folk who had witnessed the event and
none had e'er forgotten—or been the same since. Ms Podleś
touched God, and we the audience were the beneficiaries;

that's what I expect from our first sex.

Ewa's Requiem

It must be something lovely, certainly,
that night in San Francisco, when we meet:
I feel it ripple through the time continuum—
even here—now—riding the 7-train.

I expect all of my mental functions
to be entirely short-circuited—phone
lines down—flights suspended—all future dates
broken, cancelled, dissolved. I want to spend

that evening lost completely in your lap,
rocking on a tusk of ivory, my arms
clasped around your neck, my ass a wreck,
as music, moans, whatever, pours from me.

I can't see any quicker way to God
than swallowing your sperm as Ewa sings.
But will you still fuck me if I confess
I've never heard *The Requiem* of Verdi?

Green-blooded Hobgoblin

It is stagnant and sultry today on Maui, no trades, my least fave
days in the semi-tropix; I'm sipping my first cup of pu-ehr, having
just spilled piss all over the bathroom counter and floor (I was
douching out my ears); the day is off to an awkward
      start.

I don't know how to do this, this relationship thing; I've
never had a successful relationship. Which means I
don't know what works, what doesn't work; I have no
techniques, agendas or solutions. Which means I am a
baby, naked on the floor, waiting for someone to come
      feed me.

If I had Zachary Quinto, subdued in my lap, I would
share him with you. We could dress him up as Spock and
toy with his emotions. I would let you have the
first bite; I wouldn't begrudge it if he kissed you
      first.

If Zack then filched you away, to a planet on which I am
unable to breathe, I would smile benignly and whisper: *Live
long and prosper.* But would I mean it? And who would
care for all these orphaned poems? My cup is empty—I must needs a
      second cup;

You have touched me, in places that had lain dormant, and
now no breeze blows to cool the burn:
      Live long and prosper, my love.

How to Live Long and Prosper

Around the time that you were leaving school
for porn, I was starting to teach myself
how to suppress my emotions—not
my love of boys—just fooling with a few

survival techniques picked up on TV
from Mr. Spock. He taught me how to live—
half-human, pointy-eared—with aliens
I could never hope to understand.

The blue veins in my arms let me pretend
my blood was copper-based—bright green—until
I tripped down the back stairs, shattered a
window, nearly slit my carotid artery,

bleeding red all over mom. I received
six horrible sutures beneath a sheet
of light, scared that the lidocaine would turn
my rubbery face into a permanent mask.

My face recovered. That scar has faded.
But you can see it if you stand close
and raise my chin. You might also see
my eyes are green. Locked inside is Spock.

What Would Darwin Say?

I could make a case for
sex with latex marital aids as being
unnatural—but fruits and
veggies? what could be more
wholesome!

I could make a case for the consumption of
blood—were I Bill, were you Sookie—it is
nutritious, it is intimate, it is spiritual,
sustainable, and goddess knows it is
natural.

I can make a case for the infernal
internet, spooky tho it may be, which
allows two people to share their souls, in
different centuries, in galaxies far far
away.

What I cannot make a case for is this
distance between us—six-thousand
miles of brine and dust, and the fact of
this ghoulish separation we both
feel;

it just ain't natural!

Red Eye

Your e-mail says the alcohol
left you tipsier than usual.
It's made me kind of sad. Beer
can have that odd effect. Weird.

We're both a bit hammered, unfit
to operate a car, forklift,
or hearse, whatever. So, we drink
more as we attempt to shrink

great distances to cans and glasses.
Later, as the Pacific passes,
we yawn, burp, get up to pee,
look down. Back to square one. Why me?

I hear a plane descend the sky
above La Guardia. I try
to sleep. I can't. I masturbate—
shoot twice. No help. It's four. Too late

to call. I drift off to a dream,
a flight domestic in its theme.
I see a man stand at my door,
searching for keys. On the floor,

luggage: one heavy bag, one light.
He finds his keys. (Pants pocket, right.)
I hear a massive deadbolt click.
Me, I am lying on my stomach,

naked, warm, my legs a V,
and hard again—evidently
quite delighted he is here.
I pull the covers from my rear,

eyes closed. I feel him slip a hand,
between my cheeks. I think that man
must be you. That's why I groan,
"Better late than never, dick."

Nocturnal Omissions

Actually, 'twas not the alcohol's fault, for my
tipsy, but a wonky day from the Ménière's—high
pressure system or something, the gin had an almost
stabilizing effect ('twas the floor that kept
dancing);

as for the cocktail, Hendrick's is the finest gin in
the world, brewed by swarthy, red-pubed Scotsmen in
woolen skirts donning nothing beneath, with cucumber and
rose petals, as clean as a midsummer night's
piss;

the mixer, San Pellegrino Aranciata, hails straight from an
ancient citrus grove in the hills of Umbria, where hairy-
legged Umbrians smash succulent *arance* with dirty, turgid
bare feet—a ritual that has gone on since Dionysian
times;

gin itself was invented many millennia ago high in the
Himalayas, as medicine, by naked proficients in the snow, the
centuries-old junipers planted by a great blue Being named
Ginji who co-authored the Vedas and lives to this very
day.

So you see it was not the "alcohol" that was at issue—as I
proceeded to watch an Irish film in which Colin Farrell bumbled
his way between a crippled daughter and a eurotrash
selkie named *Ondine* (and who cannot watch a Colin Farrell
flick

without seeing his national flag raised proudly—if illicitly—on
the internet!); or later that evening, when I fell into a fave Lucas
Kazan scenario and imagined how you might feel upon the steamy
island sands of the Aegean: 'twas you what rocked my equi-
librium;

love is the shortest distance between any two hearts, and yet
distance is all we have thusfar known—that which stands in
 the way we might call karma—and an evening's toddy may
make the space in-between seem more ephemeral, but it does
 not,

in any sense of the imagination, put your warmth against my
skin, flood my sinuses with pheromones, or dampen my sheets and
 hair with sweet, holy emissions. Patience buys us naught but
these poems; temperance, as Blake would confer, is a cold cold
 bitch.

Burnt Fingers

I never leave a man without a souvenir—
a name, a mole, a memory, a pearl,
how dark, how light, how his sweat glands have
scattered scents about his frame like seeds

that flower into poems. In your case,
the poem has preceded you. You are
cold water on a blister here, as I
cool a burn I got when grabbing the

handle of a hot pan. I forgot
to find a good potholder, since I thought
I was grabbing you. I bet your lips
feel better on a blister though. Like ice.

Or maybe liquid nitrogen. I can
caress you safely in the dead end world
of Art, where one feels nothing really—numb.
But add a finger of flame, a lick of fire,

then frozen cries leap up off the page.

Morning Chai

I prefer to make my chai from scratch: ginger, allspice,
cinnamon stick, star anise, clove, cardamom (*LOTS* of
cardamom) all boiled together for five hours, then add a
proper Assam, sweetened with any mixture of coconut
sugar, cane sugar and honey, and a dollop of rich, heavy
cream (for want of proper yak butter);

but in the real world, there is just one of me now—no
gang, no family, no yoga ensemble—and a cup or two are
all that my diet will allow, so I use a tea bag from an
organic Indian trading company and spike it with extra
cinnamon and green cardamom powder.

Life gives us as many opportunities as it does
limitations; we grab the one and accept the other. God,
after all, holds all the keys.

I haven't made love (or had sex) in a half a decade; I find
most men shallow, arrogant, prosaic and entirely unenlightened.
Would we have overlooked each other in passing? I

wonder. But when we meet now we will have a
herstory, a project behind us, prayers uttered and an
enthusiasm for the meeting. And, yes, fear and trepidation—
fear is good.

I'm not sure that you are my "type" any more than I am
yours; but what does that mean now, now that we have
shared tears on the same ephemeral pillow? now that our
ejaculates have impregnated the cosmic whispers?

And when we meet, it will be as strangers, we will
drink heartily from the same stiff cup—ginger and
green cardamom—

and the Mystery will arise—as from the spices of our
 steaming cup.

Strange Meeting

Would we have over-looked each other
in passing—pissing at a gym urinal,
or shopping for some carrots at the store?

What a stupid question. Here we are.
My dick is thicker, thanks to you. Just like
when I stood in Waterstone's, pulled your book

off the shelf, ignoring all the others. Did
your orange cover catch my eye? Your spine?
Did something you say seize my scrotum, "You

had better take me home if you want these
back, boy." I've no idea. I just paid
my money, took you home. A whim. That choice

has altered all of my tomorrows now.
Graying—about the age I am today—
I looked at your portrait twelve years ago—

new to me as an exotic newt. Cute.
I studied your expression and compared
dust jacket photo to the words inside—

looking for insight. Here's what I learned:
your bartender is Trebor, you like Poles,
you shoot wild cats. You wrote an epitaph

that rhymes, just like John Gay. Yes, we might have
never met. We might have died a thousand ways
today. But here we are. Imagine that.

The Good News

I was late today to the gym; not my normal early-after-
noon reverie, the place was full of college-aged punks with
lithe young bodies and sweaty jerseys bearing initials and logos that
meant nothing to me. It's a good thing I don't have
esteem issues;

I pumped thinking of you, how much I would like to feel the
weight of my imaginings lunging through the emotional
sphincter of your workaday-world reality. Into a void that
feels like life, feels like death, where there are no more questions of
esteem issues.

The good news is that Jesus loves me the way that I am—and
that I lost another three pounds; now home with cats and bunnies and
gin in hand, I'm settling in to watch *Prince of Persia* and two
hours of Jake Gyllenhaal's hirsute chesticles and irrepressible
grin; it's a

good thing I don't have esteem issues. The good news is that
by the time I read naked, in five weeks, at a convention in San
Francisco, I will have lost another five pounds and be just
about where I want to be; the good news is that for the first
time ever I will be reading with a handsome—naked—young

man, you, freshly fucked from the night before, my own
dick having doubled in size overnight and my tumescent smile an
enigma of satisfaction with a trace of gloating (and if the
audience has esteem issues, fuck 'em!). You make me want to
pee from skyscrapers.

The Difference

Our spasms of orgasm past,
your cock slips slowly from my ass,
dribbling a little lube and cum,
laying its head on my scrotum—
to catch his breath, evaluate
what happens next: fuck or mate?

Nude, or naked, in a bed
I have messed up inside my head,
the question now occurs to me—
fuck or mate? It's actually
a silly question, is it not?
Love or sex, our wads are shot.

Resting on me like a kiss,
I wonder what the difference is.
The tablespoon of sperm beneath
my belly says, so I believe,
it's biological between us—
animal. That's all. My penis

nods—he agrees. My dick agrees
with everyone. Each passing breeze
excites him. But I can't ignore
love's vast complexity—how warm
I feel inside. There I get stuck:
Animals mate. I want to fuck.

Pulp Friction

I live with seven beloved kitties: Maya, Lela, Frieda; the
dudes, Rumi, Aragorn, Archimedes and Gandalf. We have
three bunnies, Beatrix, Benjamin and Alice. I've lost
count of the chickens (who keep going AWOL and raising
surreptitious clutches in the woods);

when we move to the Black Mountain farm I am
desperate for a milkable nanny and a marvelously useless
burro. I imagine a Newfoundland named Aslan and a
pug named Rasputin—or vice versa—but we shall
see who shows up.

Thing is, my life is filled with furriness and love; I have
a bevy of Facebook suitors and there's always the die-
hard fan base. And still I am a reborn virgin—after all, who
can keep up with me poetically? And then you come a-
long, a Nipponese scholar cubicle-boi with a

penchant for snarks and iambic pentameter. And did I
mention a colon that snugs over me like a Nordic fore-
skin? I am plucked, I am petted (I can hear my rooster
crowing in the back forty); I am a wand with one
singular wish:

Access to your innermost chamber.

Spoil the Child

You remind me of an Andy Goldsworthy sculpture, some-
times ephemeral—a series of colored leaves in a swirling
creek—sometimes unmovable, a granite phallus against an
incoming tide; you have become a piece of my
visionary landscape—noble, archetypal, pungent, wet.

You are the song that's irrevocably lodged in my tune-
repeater—classic Flatt & Scruggs—romantic, comical, full of
piss and vinegar; and no matter how dedicated my nap, or
meditation, or attempt at any work, I find that I simply
can't stop dancing.

You remind me of my Grandma. Not because you smell like
Juicy Fruit gum—I don't know that yet—but because no matter
how grim or uptight my day, there's always cookies and
cake lurking just around the corner;

but unlike Grandma, I know better than to spare the rod. After
all: *a bottom well-fed*
       keeps to its own bed.

Out of Doors

Not being a sleepwalker by nature, I
seldom find myself wandering into brick
shithouses by moonlight. I will drop by
the fridge to gnaw on a cold drumstick—

now and then—seized by hunger pangs—
the result of the treadmill. I've been doing
so much running. I want to look good for you
in Cali, or Black Mountain, wherever

pale asses glow most poetically by night.
I am thinking of myself here. I see
me—for no good reason—because I am
incarcerated in a gray cubicle—

abandoning treadmills for roads—doing
dirty things out doors: lying under
a tree, sharing a green sleeping bag—
well-fed, well-fucked—well, wondering if

this sort of life would make me happy—
if, God forbid, my fantasies came true.

Of Asses and Ashes

My nobler self wants to say "Relax, I love you just the
way you are," but my more prurient (and often domi-
nant) voice mutters "Fuck no, tight and trim is good"—after
all, I'm doing the same thing for you (having fun with it, and
most grateful for the motivator);

and as the senior member of this alliance, I demand free and
unqualified access to your every hair and follicle, lubri-
cation will be applied at my total discretion, and un-
authorized shaving of body parts is cause for immediate
dismissal;

that said, you may do anything you want *to me* any
time, any place, and as often as you like. (Just keep in mind I am a
true Clintonian—oral is foreplay, not sex.)

Why be coy, we don't know each other, and tho sex will
certainly not sustain the relationship, it will be a fun and
important coming-together, and I want all cogs and
pipes fitted and greased for maximum play. After that, we
scour the ashes for pearls and lost watches and

evaluate what we have left: I have a hole in my life that
you might fill brilliantly. As for anything resembling a
marriage—we should probably do brunch first. And
as for that other matter, perhaps some modifications in the
types of protein might make for a difference;

I'm a true southerner, I promise you won't go hungry.

Ashes to Asses, Dust to Lust

Don't misunderstand me, dear. I'm wed
to speculation, for our future is
not carved in stone. If my tight fanny fits
atop your cock, or it buckles, we shall

learn. For morning to exist in any form—
a gentle lay at dawn or Bloody Mary
at brunch—we must reserve a seat—at least
have a destination in mind. I have come

home from brunch, to find my house burning,
a smoke choked sky, and, to my astonishment,
laughed, lit a cigarette, happy I was
full and carried a toothbrush in my bag.

When the police allowed me back inside,
I cried a bit—it's true—my windows smashed,
bed glittering with glass, that day destroyed.
At least I was insured for fire. I found

no pearls among my debris, just CDs.
I open cases now—15 years
later—to find dead musicians veiled
in soot. Unplayable discs. These I replace

with new recordings. Life goes on.

Urine My Thoughts

Speculation leads to uncertainty, un-
certainty to doubt; what I am certain a-
bout is that there is a poem in us, just
waiting to break out. *(Forgive me Calliope, for
I have rhymed ....)*

What I am certain about is that the foto I have of you in
your sock hat and glasses, in front of the Imperial
Palace @ Tokyo—and looking so much like a hand-
some young Ken Wilbur—makes me want to open your
covers and read you to the spine;

what I am certain about is that this shot of your flexed
armpit makes me want to count every hair upon
your body and arrange them into varying brocades and
demeanors with my tongue;

and the close-up of your disarmingly callipygian but-
tocks makes me want to swan dive into the depths of
succulent abyss, to never return for air;

I am certain that your jawline, as depicted unshaved, will
give me more pleasure to gnaw than any serving from our
president's overrated Asheville rib-joint;

I am certain that this poetic collaboration shall be a-
mong the great achievements of my life, and that the only
greater achievement would be to call you my lover my
disciple my wife *(damn rhymes ...);*

what I am certain about is that I want to pick you
up like a warm German stein and drink your steaming
contents to the last frothing gulp—thereby putting you to

bed with a thousand kisses and a grin on every
  orifice;

  what I am certain of is that I wish to sleep at night with
your musk in my nostrils and the salts of your piss on my
  tongue, and that when I open my eyes your grumpy mum-
bling is the
          lark of my dawn.

Shopping

Buying vegetables this morning, the gems
adorning the pale bulbs of kohlrabi grabbed
my eyes—like stars. Oh, just water droplets, to
be sure, a mist, but they were magical—love-
ly—the way rain shafts shimmer, when they
catch the sun and shatter into a million
colors. Cucumbers, beet greens with ruby stems,
cauliflower, carrots, radishes—the asparagus!
Everything was wet, gorgeous, delicious, and I
thought of all the wonders we might work together
in the kitchen—the delicate dishes—the sauces—
the béarnaise! I pulled a leaf of tarragon from
a bundle, rolled it between my thumb and fore-
finger, so my skin picked up the scent, and
I sniffed my fingertips for you. How fresh!

'Tain't Fair!

This crappy video, of your privates, your wobblies, your
'tain't, makes me swoon, dear. I who abhor porn—but who
adore you—sipping on Hendrick's and watching you
bend toward your cam again and again and again, wink-
ing at me like a forest creature from a branch, furry for

winter and safe at a distance; I would net you or
bag you with my .22—no, not that, I need you breathing and
trembling with trepidation—careful not to scratch you or
get scratched, calming and soothing and yet knowing that I
lie, that I want to grasp and abuse you:

"Bend over, bitch, show me China;
spread your cheeks and say Ahhhhhhh …
there, now doesn't that feel better?
Daddy's home, you have
nothing to fear!"

*   *   *   *   *

My dear, I fear you've made me hotter than I
really am: handsome men are coming on to me, young
men, sexy men, men with followings of their
own; like today, the tree guy, come to remove a chunk of a
Java plum that crashed down against my dome during the

last storm; Emile climbed and chainsawed—I hauled
away the remnants—Emile is porn-star hot—and yes I
tipped him, for a not-quite-two-hour job—but he
hugged me goodbye, and sweaty thank-you, there were
tears in his eyes;

it's YOU, it's this damn video of you that makes my
pubic areas emit scents that yowl of the rut; puppies are
 following me down sidewalks, men and women of all ages are
peeling the clothes from my hyper-alert form—and all I
 want is you, spread-eagle before me,

quaking, homeless, and needing to be
        tamed.

A Dog's Life

I can't take this anymore—I'm sore—
leave me alone—get out of my head!
I closed my eyes five times today, felt you
knocking wildly against my prostate—as if
my prostate were my heart—spurting soul

each time I came. I licked my fingers to
replenish my insides. I am a husk.
My skin seems alien. I can't touch myself,
even to wash, without feeling your
hands holding the soap. When standing

before the mirror after swimming, I
squirt moisturizing cream into my palm,
bend over, rub my shins, my knees, my thighs,
my muscles stiffen, like a giant cock
I am stroking in public. My body

must belong to you. I am a dog,
a Victor dog, a werewolf spinning round
in circles to the sound of a new voice.
Whatever crazy music you desire
to hear me howling at the moon, I play.

Five Tanka in the Form of Ono no Komachi

Classic Maui evening, greenhouse frogs
mimic the soughing of the trades—
were you here, the moonless sky would shine
brightly upon your shoulders, these sultry
frogs hushed in completion.

*   *   *

Where does winter begin and
autumn end?
your imagined touch
burns more hotly
than it should.

*   *   *

I should be off, this quiet hour, to
floss and brush my teeth,
but find my vigil by the phone,
as if your sleepy voice
were at the other end.

*   *   *

Rainy tropical morning, strong
pot of oolong and a
 woody full of piss—
you should be here, to
 share in these fluids.

*   *   *

Silk shorts on a chilly wet day,
the clamoring of the gutters,
 pearls on my
fist for the
 want of you.

Dawn

This morning I awoke to a strange shade—
a pink without parallel—a new one.
I lay there studying the shadows made
by cherry trees in my imagination.
Limbs danced on window blinds—my mind—a fan
hiding a Noh player, a young man,
performing for his Shogun on a stage—
not cherry—darker wood. But the image—
flirtatious as it was—as all Art is—
seemed so substantial! No telephones
rang, no sirens screamed, no thumps, no groans
excited curiosity, no his-
sing radiator ventilated steam;
nothing—not a whisper—intervened

to disturb my universe. You lay
six thousand miles away. I tied my shoes,
sad I had to spend the rest of my day
surrounded by cruel colors: glass blues
rising from Manhattan like tsunami!
Give me Basho, Ono no Komachi!
Let me suspend the world in clouds of pink
so soft cherry blossoms on the brink
would close their eyes unable to resist
repeating, "This is Heaven. Where I land
is immaterial. I'll have one hand
in Heaven always." In lieu of a kiss
this morning, take a poem—floating there
forever. Words are all I have to share.

Prayer

I've been having my teeth whitened—five shades
whiter so far, just one shade to go; I've lost
five pounds, four more to go to my perfect
weight; I am finishing up my tattoos (will they
ever be finished?); and am having a

missing tooth replaced with a bionic implant ...
and still, no matter what I do, I can never be any
younger than 55, and you will always always be
fifteen years my junior (does that give *me* the
advantage, or you?); and altho my

body is about as perfect as a 55 y/o body can
possibly be, you will always have a firmer de-
riere, (thank Goddess I have a full head of
hair, albeit white unto my very pubes ...); as for
who remains hardest and hardest longest, the

jury is still out. Perhaps it is perfect that you're
a pixie slut and I'm the lascivious mentor—tho
which is the most wanton might be a
question for the ages; I am thrilled that at
least of lust and verse we are of a

heated match. My favorite line of Lao Tzu is
that "the softest thing in the universe over-
comes the hardest thing in the universe"—with-
out love to bind us we are just a stirring of
dust, which the winds of time will

scatter beyond a trace; with love we are a
force of nature, and will bend the creation to our
desires. And yet Spirit trumps all—I want to
ride you into Nothingness, leaving these time-

sensitive thought-bodies behind, and join the

ranks of Blessed Lovers who have become
etched in the nighttime sky—Rumi and Shams,
Jonathan and David, Francis and Claire—we
are the lips that pray
     I Am.

A Matter of Belief

I'm not a praying man,
ordinarily, though I can-
not hear prayer and not
be moved to bow,
a little, humbled by
the beauty of the gesture—
envious of the belief
the cosmos cares about
what I desire. Lord,

how many times I have
looked up and heard
no answers, nothing, noise—
a yippy Chihuahua,
my fridge compressor,
somebody cumming
copiously upstairs—
calling out to—Heaven
knows. Certainly not me.

Not you. Unless your
middle name is
God—not Geoffrey.

Logos

I can teach you how to love each and every one of my seven
kitties—for they all have quite different requirements and
triggers—but I cannot instruct you how to make love to
me, for I have lost that connection and must rely on you to
find it for me/us;

I had buffalo dogs today—not because you are from
Buffalo, but because buffalo meat is genetically purer and
thusly better for us than beef or pork; for in nature there be
secrets that exist in the very cells of our bodies that
open doors and pathways we for lifetimes have for-

gotten about. I think you can teach me how to be
me again; the mentor bows before the student and all is
revealed. It is in your voice when you call me "Sir
Goat" … it is in your saliva when you lick my
hand; do not be

afraid of what stands before you—too naked for
most—for Spirit has chosen you, to be the Vessel, to
be the Activator, Love Made Flesh, the
Poem, the Pause in-Between the Poems, my Pet, my
Keeper, my

Logos.

The Art of Desire

Buddhist or Hindu underlings will tell you that you
must lose your desires to awaken. This is not true, tho it
 may be part of a path to some; the quickest way to enlighten-
ment is simply to wake up. *Be* God (as opposed to
"think God" or just-say-you're-God the way the

New-Agers do); desire is simply desire, it is like
hunger, it is a manifestation of carnal "reality" and
 not the source of bondage (ignorance is); desire be-
gets disappointment and anger and grief, and these
too are merely a facet of being

human. Know God and all these things are simply
theatre. And desire is, well, desire, as enjoyable and
 fulfillable and disappointable and enpassionable as is
hunger before a Thanksgiving feast … or yearning be-
for making love. So relax, be aware, and en-

Joy;
and desire me, for I will fill you as long as the
Goddess allows.

      *   *   *   *   *

I was supposed to watch some professorial DVD this
evening, some philosophical-slash-quantum-phy-
 sical yadada yadada lecture series, but instead—and
being more than a little bit drunk and so preferring
warm-and-fuzzy—I

plopped on *The History Boys* for my 47th
viewing; I hate these fucking time zones, where a-

bout the time I'm feeling perky and ready for
play, you, my erudite lad, my noetical li-
  brarian, are sighing dreamily in your

bed six-thousand miles away—and so here I am, as
ever, coming down off my buzz and stacking up
poems—"lit'rature" "philosophy" "sublimation" "ex-
cuses" … and what else have I to do, ancient poet-
monk in want of an elfin scholar?

I love *The History Boys*, it makes me happy—it
always makes me happy—as do you, o sleeping
  sonnet, as does Hendrick's gin, and melted goat
cheese on a half an English muffin; you are the
rose outside my window—"Heirloom"—and

when this winter is over and spring breaks upon us, I
plan to race outside, bathrobe and slippers asunder, and
  bury my face in your lovely, brilliant, fragrant, color-
filled petals, and breathe of your shocking presence un-
til I can no more distinguish the

nose from the rose.

      *   *   *   *   *

One of the popular contemporary gurus said (and it
helps to read this with an Indian accent) something to the
  effect of: *The problem is not desire, the problem is in
not getting that which we desire.* Well … no,
  neither of these is the problem;

suffering comes from being attached to the end re-
sult. It's a matter of intensity; desire is desire, and
  disappointment is just that. My Guru says "I work like
hell for what I want, then I accept what God gives
  me." Fortitude, Patience, Temperance,

Surrender. We have planted a seed, you and I, but we
cannot predict the tree that it will become. But what fun we
can have pissing on its roots, dancing around its
trunk, and (with God's blessing) someday cradling in its
arms.

Fresh Ink

Four hours tonight at the tattoo shop—two hours just
aligning six elephants in their proper positions around the
 yin/yang upon my left shoulder, trunk to tail; two
hours or so under the needle, drinking nasty local coco-
 nut beer with Circle, our island's most-accomplished

 artist. You were on my mind—that and an annoying Police
song—it may have been the pain, but more
 likely the interior space beneath the pain ... you with
your succulent white flesh unfettered by pachy-
 derms or teeth marks; I would never

 suggest that you take the plunge, but all the same do
wish you the joy of the pain of a job well-done, a
 night well-loved, and the stain of a lover's brutal
ink splayed across your raw young
 canvass.

Invisible Ink

According to *The Telegraph*—
September 21st, 2010—
in World War I, a lad
at London University learned
semen makes excellent ink for
secret messages: seminal
fluids don't react to iodine
vapor, the standard chemical
tests, and gentlemen—spies,
prisoners, lovers—always
have access to fresh supplies—
fresh being the operative
word. Spunk can't be stored
in the field very conveniently:
it quickly starts to stink,
giving the army away. If this
emboldened our boy to jack-
off in his lab and start
scribbling, the article didn't say.
Nor did it reveal his name.
I suspect this patriot wrote
poetry in his spare time.

I remembered all this
this morning, reading about
your new tattoos. I pictured you—
beautifully bareback—
just yesterday, facedown,
under a hot, bright lamp,
a needle buzzing, you wincing a
bit, maybe, sipping a warm
bottle of disgusting beer—
as Circle, the artist,
inscribed a pachyderm

prancing proudly on your arm.
I also pictured myself
next month—biting
a pillow—my mouth full of
goose down. I wonder
what kind of marks your
teeth will leave on my
pale shoulders? What secret
messages—what poetry—
will you pick up your
pen to write? And how
will I feel afterwards,
when I can read your thoughts?
Will I regret that night?

The Sound of One Pen Scribbling

Nice poem, Munchkin. Nice images and reference. Of
course I picture Jamie McAvoy, on the battlefield in
Atonement, carefully preparing his secret epistle to Keira
Knightly; then I imagine Ewan McGregor adorned only in
kanji in *Pillow Book* ... and then

James scripting calligraphically upon Ewan, directly from his
artful pen ... no, wait!—pan back to poets Eric and Gav in an
heroically literary montage against the white cliffs of
Dover ... upon the misty moss gardens at Kyoto ... atop a hay
stack in a decrepit barn in Black Mountain, North

Carolina ... and already my oolong has gone empty ...

Ah! reloaded—picture our heroes high atop a Formosa
tea plantation, the master Gavsho stuffing his dirty, Camellia
sinensis-stained fingers in the novice poet Ericyo's thirsting
mouth, prodding his writhing form for heretofore
undisclosed manuscripts, a

frantic dance of passion, caffeine, and mumbled meta-
phors ...

the Truth is: I want to recite you like a
mantra, and write illusion-shattering
koans upon the parchment of
your throbbing hot
prostate.

4 Koans

A single pen
scribbling does not
a poem make, although
a poet may contain
a multitude.

Your soul remains
more ink to me
than man: something
liquid I can
hold, like hope.

When I am tired,
my language sharp,
the mantra which
my heart repeats
is very soft—

so listen close.
Put your ear
against the phone
and close your eyes:
the sounds of home.

Into the Woods

I wore a wife-beater out in public today, for the first time in
some years—the diet has worked—and I confess I got
looks and comments both. I could score pretty well for a
55-year-old, were I in the market; but you and I know
better, for I am a

cranky old hermit/wizard that prefers the ways of ents and
elves to the giddy, unconscious plays of man and orc—my
hair is white, my skin, where it is not inked, lined and
scarred from battles both lost and won; and adventure to
me is sitting unmoved upon a rock until

squirrels, deer, skunks and snakes find me useful as both
pillow and perch. But you, precocious halfling, when you
grin and dance before me, even the possums mumble how
tasty you might be in a pie or stew—and it becomes im-
possible to not feed you peanuts and

wonder how you might feel at the foot of my bed.

How I See You

Today, I saw a hunk in a wife-beater in
a picture, posing, freshly inked. His purple
elephants, linked trunk to tail, still looked
a little painful, pink, raw and tender
in places. Who was he? He looked like you.

No, not Gavin Geoffrey, in the flesh,
undressing for success—another you.
The tuft of armpit there, against your wife-
beating white, didn't arouse those elephants,
though it affected parts of me. Tonight,

before I went to bed, I looked through all
the photos I possessed of you—younger,
older, picking out my favorite. You
sit beside a gorgeous Grammatophyllum,
wearing a black hoodie and glasses.

You'll think I am crazy, but I can read
through your lenses better than you—what
is written there around your eyes by Time—
the poetry of God or Fate—whatever
name we assign the genius with the pen.

That man is mine. Remove it all—the frames,
the hoodie, orchid, elephants, old
and new tattoos—there's my Naked Poet:
all that you are, just as you appear.
The essential man. So essential to me.

To See or Not to See

The light quality in the video is dismal, dark, grainy, al-
most solarized at times; the figure is neither short nor
tall—there are no reference points. The man's jaw is
wide and strong, tho the chin short and uncertain; his
eyes are undisclosed.

Too much information scares us—we are creatures of
Mystery—and perhaps that is Wisdom, for information is
usually misleading; the cock is dark, tho briefly seen in
silhouette as the body twists; shoulders, biceps, thighs all
show of tone and muscle; the

waistline is precious and wants to be firmly held. And
then the figure turns, the rump flares in profile only to
wiggle into place before the intruding lens—as I said, the
film is too dark for intimate disclosure, it is a hint, a
teaser, a phantom for the digitally inclined.

We are frightening ourselves with expectations, all this
poetic nuance toward marriage and eternality; I am more than a
half-century old and, though I have hailed numerous
astounding relationships, have never had one successful
marriage—too much the poet, I

fear. Still, I am yet a child, and have left every door and
window open—indeed the walls themselves have become
tenuous—for who can predict God's illustrious designs?
Love is eternal, and the degree to which we surrender does
secure our pages in Perpetuum. You once

jested, "Jesus saves, but I put out"—I cannot tell you how
much I look forward to plundering all your furry places; you said
Yes to reading naked with me in SF, with hardly a hiccup for

thought—you have never even set foot in California ... *balls!* (from a
 shadowy image to the public stage!).

 It is a rainy night on Maui, you are asleep a million miles
away—your every breath brings me closer to your lips;
 we are the portals of the Unknowable, you and I, the hapless
slaves of eternity; one last glance at the dancing chimera in the
 film clip and I
          wank myself to sleep.

The Collaborators

Chimeras, slaves, or funny faces,
what we are, we must become
together. Kissing cousins, friends,
lovers, bitter disappointments, they
color all our sunsets. And yet,

the more I talk to you, the more
I walk around my neighborhood
until my poor iPhone drops dead—
its batteries exhausted—the more
those sunsets seem irrelevant.

Some days ago, I can't think when,
or what I must have said, you placed
your fingers on a key, pressed send,
applied some gentle pressure. We
ceased to write separate poems

then. I responded to your words.
My heart, stupid muscle head he is,
continued pumping iron. I didn't skip
a single meal. Nor did my bowels
stop moving out of reverence for you.

The only thing I noticed was
the way that I viewed paper had
changed. Everything was different.
Then, this page became a bed
where you and I could screw forever.

I Want to

be codependent with you; I want to
get drunk and operate heavy equipment;
I want to seek counseling together and then
gang up on the counselor until he
calls the cops—I want to

belligerate the cops. I want to ride in-
to the dusk with you, guns blazing against the
crepuscular desert horizon—your
sphincter is my stirrup; I want the Madonna and
Lady Gaga fans of the world to

stand up, point at us and say "They're
not one of us!"; I want to attempt to smuggle a
quart jar of our semens past the NSA at the
airport and then explain that it will make the
plane go faster; I want us to

defend the poor against Christian values, po-
litical posturing, veganism, Microsoft Word and
all things evil—we are the masked duo, wet be-
neath our spandex codpieces, and no one
knows the secret fluids we inhale nightly, if only

to enrage those hags at MADD.

Us

We must be mutants then. The DNA
tests confirm it. And our love for combat
boots, angora sweaters, animals,
the ones we used to fuck like mad, but now
we must feed. We are nurses. We can

handle nukes in nylons. We absorb
cosmic rays. We write poems and plays
that baffle all the critics because love,
like life, is so damn baffling. Shakespeare
would understand us. Sappho. Housman.

Housman the best. Dog and cat lovers.
Apple people. Adam. Eve. I believe
a lad I liked and almost slept with once—
named Steve—no relation to the saint
I kissed goodbye and never saw again.

Who are we then? We few, that happy few,
the lucky ones, that band of others, who
stood at Stonewall, Dunkirk, and Thermopylae
against barbarians. We are their tongues,
lungs, vocal cords—the voices of the dead.

We are unlikely heroes, you and I:
naked, standing up against the sky.

Deus Caritas est

The status quo is afraid of those who Love—always
has it been so; lovers defy property rights, lovers reject
income, lovers traverse every boundary;

as long as homosexuals are demonized (or, *some*one
is demonized), the Bushes and Rockefellers of this
world can cross oceans to bomb sand-niggers;

we are the radicals who claim sperm-not-blood, we
are the monks who claim Spirit, not dogma; we are the
Christs who continue to die for their ignorance;

and so we are the Blessed who touch Love and are
touched back, you are the Truth the Light and the
Way, to drink from the pit of your arm is a

sacrament of the ages; we have transmuted water into
Wine, blood into Stardust, dust unto Eternity—the
Honey from your lips shall sustain me in this

desert, until such a time as we
        sit naked upon the knees of Jesus.

Strange Lights

Don't think me cynical
if I find love incredible—
miraculous as that
distant day I first
heard it described in
the salty language sailors use
by a man I met inside
a misty waterfront tavern.
I stood a round of drinks to
hear his spectacular stories—
reports of fire dancing—
mastheads at midnight—
the South China Sea—
the center of violent typhoons.

I've read of love in shady
journals: strange reports—
couples coupling in cars
parked in desolate areas
seeing inexplicable lights
emanating from above.
Some say they were kidnapped
by cold-fingered aliens,
intimately probed,
then quietly returned to earth,
anesthetized. Still,
I have yet to see one
souvenir pillow
embroidered "Andromeda."

The most credible account
I've found occurs inside
the Chronicles of Canterbury.
There, before the Feast

of St. John the Baptist,
in the year 1178,
five monks witnessed a
large meteor strike the moon:
its horns split in two—
spewing molten rock into
outer space. This is
recorded by Gervase,
a reliable historian.
A man of God.

I think of myself when
I think of Gervase;
I think of strange lights when
I think of you. Clearly,
love is a celestial
event. You even
lead me to believe
all these stories are true.

Eternally Yours

Believe, my Shropshire lad, believe! for I have
seen the Lights, here on Maui, in Joshua Tree, in
Asheville (where as a teen I was taken aboard an
Andromedan triangular ship) and in Sedona; on
Mount Shasta I embraced a gentleman from Orion—he
didn't speak, but wept on my shoulder, and smelled
medicinal, like stewed garlic;

Orson Scott Card said "We are the stories we
tell about ourselves"—Orson is a Mormon, of
course, and not prone toward spirituality, yet on a
purely carnal level he is not incorrect; the trick is to
actively create our tale—as opposed to

the sheeple, who live purely in reaction; we are
the gods who come to Earth, shine brightly for a
time, then take our place in the heavens for
future generations to name and navigate from; you and
me, angel, copulating for all

Eternity.

Thru the Glass Brightly

Mon Pet,
nothing in this world irritates me more than
 securing a flight—the system is geared toward
inhospitability, humiliation and failure—I would
 rather chew razor blades in hell, or

bleed to death in a Walmart. That said, I am in
theory one step closer to feeling your breath in my
 ear and your saliva on my thigh; I am booked to
Oakland and our rendezvous. It is not the
 flight I had hoped—of course—but it is the

one that will bring us together. I see pieces of
you, the way the five blind men view the ele-
 phant, the voice, the serious fotos, the campy and
sexual videos, the poems and the prose—alas, I have
 the dearth of smell, my most pronounced

sense—and all these disparate parts revolve like
shards of colored glass in a kaleidoscope, forming ran-
 dom patterns and glimpses of a being I have yet to
grok; yet it is the eye of the spiraling fragments that
 holds me the closest and tightest—it is your

soul that whispers my name.

Mr. Smith Will Say a Few Words

Angelic as I am, you must understand,
I never have a problem booking flights
anywhere—the Moon, Uranus, Black Holes—
or, closer to home, volcanic island
chains where hairy hermits peer into caldera.
Since my wings are telepathic, I have

adopted this pseudonym Smith—Valentine
Michael Smith, to be exact. You see, I am
a stranger in the strangest land—your head.
When you're asleep, drooling, I will enter
your room, your kaleidoscopic dreams, not through
the sanitary filters of art. I enter as

myself, an alien, tainted by human textures,
smells, and customs foreign to your house.
I may come with a tinkling glass of ice-water,
leaving it on the nightstand—just in case
you wake up feeling thirsty. I may come with
more than water, too. You never know

precisely what a telepathic angel will do.

Krsna's Bitch

Make mine a gin-and-OJ, then, O Wingéd One, water
only makes me thirsty. Spoon in beside me—I love a
man what wets the bed—I know your type: angels
are all sluts, the Bible tells us so; bring me news from
distant Orion's belt, Andromeda and the Pleiades, the

lands from which Angels cometh. I am the Illustrated
Man, crawl into my skin (like a Centaurian slug) and
stain me with Holy Ink—designs of worlds my poor
beleaguered DNA has long forgotten; open mine eyes and
show me the follicles of Eternity; I promise to

show to you the hospitality that Lot showed to his
visitors—with perks!—for I am Mira, awaiting her
Dark Lord, palms upward for the Holy Sacrament, my
womb the mystic cave where Hermits dwell in
perpetuity, supplicants for the visitation of our

Makers.
Come quickly, Dark One; swoon me, consume my
heart, obliterate my last feeble thoughts in the fiery
rains of Krsna's dance; allow me to be the
rug beneath your Precious Bejeweled Feet!

Lost and Found

Love is not a spark, it is a blaze, a fire that
rages and cannot be contained until all becomes
silence beneath its ashy snow; I know I know, we
are not in love, you and I, but I can tell that
you, like I, have a fancy for matches.

In India the saddhus smear their naked bodies with
ash; it is thought to be symbolic of their tem-
porary life here in the body, but ask any saddhu and
he will tell you the truth: it keeps the mosquitoes
off when running bare-assed thru the

jungle: love is practical, after all, and follows the
forms and conventions of nature (not man). We
are two mosquitoes, you and I, banging angrily a-
gainst the same glass: you trying to get in, me
determined to get out; the glass is but

space and time—feeble space and time—which
even now are trembling between the violence of our
words our desires our curses, soon to burst, like a
bubble on a summer breeze, leaving naught but an
open window. Love is a

window with no glass, no frame, no going into nor
going out, no inside no outside, no walls and no
house; and those who go there meet themselves a-
long the road, and those who go are for-
ever lost among the Found.

Keys

Whenever I lose something, matches, keys,
glasses, building passes, they always
turn up in the last place I look,
as if they were always there—
tapping fingernails, waiting to be found,
even though I know they weren't
really sitting on the fridge, laughing
at me behind my bananas. How strangely

trans-dimensional love is. It is
something material you mislay, or lose,
like your virginity, then spend your life
searching for, under a flickering streetlamp,
at night, because the light is better there—
on the street—than in the alley where
you really think you lost it—lost
everything—keys, glasses, and virginity.

Imagine me then. Here you come, while
I'm on all fours, jeans round my ankles,
frantically patting the pavement, bare-assed.
You say, "Dude, dude, why the hell
are you kneeling in the gutter?" I say, "I can't
find my keys." You look at me, dumbfounded
for a moment. But you understand.
"Um," you say, "Dude, you asked me to

hold on to them while we were fucking.
You were about to come when you ran off.
I came to bring you back upstairs."

The Hornéd One

It's no street trick, reaching down your
throat and pulling out your heart, hell you were
already choking on it; I heard your prayers:

> *Dear Siva, love your postcards and teeshirts and*
> *stuff; you have some really great merchandisers*
> *down here. God is good; I think you're hot;*
> *blue is beautiful.*
> *Facebook me?*

If you don't see me as Siva, look again:
vipers dive into my body, as horns
 sprout out like warts;
the mighty Ganges flows from the
 crack in my skull and floods
the plains beneath me;
 with Durga on one palm and Kali on the
other, I can seduce the world and lay it to
 ruin, riding away on my sacred mount,
with the flick of a tail we are vanished:
 lie down before me and weep, for all that you
have imagined is true, and all you have
 dreamed is laid to waste;
I am Siva—
Who did you think you were messin' with?

Now, little boy, if you would, I have
universes to attend to. So
 pick up your damn keys, pull up your
trousers,
 and let's go Home.

A Prayer to Siva

Thunder, thunder, thunder.
Bitch, bitch, bitch.
What kind of performance is this?
Here I am prostrate before you—
all humility—my
ass quivering in the air,
the perfectly submissive creature.
What do you do? You bitch.
You topple empires, skip galaxies
across time and space like
flat rocks across a pond.
Lord, it must be boring
out there in the universe.
Next thing you know you'll start
pulling wings off flies. What

a strange god you are.
Look, Siva, before
you draw a black line through
Creation, or, on second thought,
crumple the whole thing
up, toss it over your
great shoulders, like so
much waste paper, why don't
you take a lesson from
Zeus? Just drop by in a shower
of gold—for a good time?
Just you and me. Why not
make it tonight? The stars do not
need you as much I do.
Loved or unloved, up there,
they will continue to shine.

Blissfully Yours

My Diminutive Arjuna, do you not know that
we have made love since before the first
   epoch roiled into existence? do you not recall my
teeth upon your neck, my haunches above yours as
the first dawn blazed across the Milky

Way? or you, with the head of a lion and the
strapping body of a griffin sliding blithely along
   Orion's belt, my vulcanized feathers in comet-like
pursuit? It was the flames of your loins that
progenitored the first super-

nova—lovingly known up in these parts as
Eric's Sphincter. It is only your mortal amnesia that
   creates such forgetting—we have played this
game a million times throughout the ages, until
   one of us or the other is touched in a

   dream in the night: a kiss from above, talons
in the dark, a breath of fire, a vision that leaves
   one's chest exploding, or a dawn finding one's
bed full of down and milky tears across the
   nape of the back. Be patient my

Eternal Love, for the millennia are our
playground and these nights alone but blinks with-
   in the ethers of our unending consummation;
you are my Heart, and there is no god, no
   demon, no apocalypse that can

   rend us apart. So tonight, as your city shudders in
yearning and expectation, as loneliness howls
   from the streets below and profoundest silence rains

from above, feel me inside you, flooding you with
the flames of creation itself, as we

ignite, once again and always and forever, in
Immortal Bliss.

My lust for you sustains me ...
priapicly yours,

Caper Caelestis

Future Perfect

Religion, my dearest hobbit, we know is a sham; from the
second a prophet's eyes are closed it is nothing but a
power grab; ultimately, religion is a shield to obfuscate
God from man, the way our brain acts to defend us against
True Knowledge; religion

is a contract with the devil, stating that we must never ever
converse directly with That Which Is; religion is real es-
tate, arbitrary lines drawn in the sand across which we
dare not step; religion is the antichrist, the brother of
politics, the sister of economics.

God, my friend, is Love, and no boundaries shall e'er
apply—no murders committed, no properties seized, no
libraries burned, and no boxes prescribed; what Lover—
what True Lover—has made limitation his home? Love, rather,
is the upturning of the bankers, the

transmutation of scripture into verse, the knocking
down of walls of church and state, the desecration of the
forms and functions of man with the adoration of the forms and
ephemera of Nature; Love is poetry not prose, nakedness not
clothes; Love is the Bliss within the Rose.

And you, my succulent cherubim, you are the perfected
vehicle, the garden to be plowed, the vessel to be
filled, adorned and adored. You are the constellation that
guides me, the ocean that cradles, and the land to
which I sail; I am a

stranger in a strange land,
but all I see is
God's Beloved Hand.

The Time Traveler's Knife

Let us pretend for a moment that time is not
linear—because in fact it is not, it telescopes out in
every direction—and that we (you and I, my
friend) have already met, are getting to know each
other, have lived long together, have held hands while

realities have shifted to another dimension ... *"chrono-
impairment,"* Dr Kendrick calls it; in the scheme of
things we have made love a zillion times and
strewn our seed throughout the Cosmos. What would be
gained from knowing the whys and the

wherefores, the hows and the how-nots? Are we
not Lovers? do we not share the same breath on the
same pillow night after night, epoch after epoch, thru
floods and famine and, indeed, immolation at the
final contraction back into

Cosmic Heart? And what of it that we have yet
to meet—when we are already united? of what
limitation is space to those who have surfed the
expansion from Singularity Point One? We are the
Cause and the Effect, the carriers of the

Flame, the wielders of the Blade of Love, which
cuts thru time and space, emptiness and
fullness, loneliness and unification, to which
angels, demons, and the spheres of the
universe bow down,

as if before God Himself.

How to Write a Romance: Backwards

Time is non-linear. Cause and effect
reflect a thoughtless habit. There's no law
that says when you or I begin a book
we can't start writing it from the rear-end.

True, there are physicists who may object.
They might suggest that we have stacked the deck
in favor of a certain outcome. Well,
perhaps we have. But what is wrong with that?

We're poets, not professors, you and I,
a pair of horny homosexuals, crazed
with lust. We were not born to gather dust
or chew up books in basements, like rats.

I'm glad you started munching on my butt—
by butt, I mean those photographs I sent—
instead of slowly plodding through my whole
biography to understand me. Now,

the poetry awaits discovery:
the scent of citrus soap combined with sweat,
the tangy taste of something on your tongue
implicit in those naked pictures. No,

nothing is pre-ordained. You take that chance.
You asked me to remove my underpants.
I did. Then we continued writing, knowing
full well how the story would turn out.

Dick First, Queries Later

As the "Naked Poet," I became used to putting my
junk before my stuff; standing naked before
 audiences gave me the edge—I came in with nothing
to conceal; having at one time been the #1 queer
 porn star, I got used to meeting people who had

long before met me—it's hard to chase a rabbit that's
not running. As a lonely and addlepated old monk on a
 farm in Yosemite, a cabin on the coast of Marin, a
shack in the Maui rainforest, I have reacquainted with
 anonymity—only the deer, the cats, the

mongoose are around to watch me pee in the
morning. And then there was you—spirit in the
 dark; pixie poet in the ethers—sending me all
your nasty funk, your wagging tail, your
 dripping tongue; hell yes we're gonna

fuck—it's been half a decade since my last! But
do not think this tryst a carnal mishap, or com-
 pulsive homo hookup; I have waited long and (*er*)
hard for this moment—like a forest creature en-
 slaved to the rut—not to mate for life, not to

procreate or architect a nest, but for the poems we
may find under leaf and log, the rhymes we may
 render in flurry and fog, the rhythms we wend as we
dance and jog ... and the metaphors to which we
 are so hap'ly enslaved. —Love? I think the love is in the

writing. —A life together? we have a publisher already
committed! Our saliva has already mingled, our
 fur entwined, our semen combined; we are coauthors of the
world's first kiss—why question this?
 Ecstasy becomes us.

The Camel

The love is in the writing, yes. It is
this pencil—architect of all my hopes.
I suck on my eraser, like a nipple.
The friction of the lead provides some heat.
The little squiggles that adorn my man-
uscript swim wonderfully between the
lines, like freshly ejected sperm,
seeking, out of instinct, a nice, warm
place they can kick off their flippers,
crack a Michelob, exhausted, and unwind.
A mouth, a hand, some other place. Who knows?

Your last poem mentioned your career,
retiring from porn, continuing to appear
naked, reading poetry in California.
I was in college then, learning from dad
sucking cock was probably something
a boy in Buffalo ought not to do.
Soon after he discovered my diary,
I found myself searching for a butt one
night along the shoulder of a road
so dark it seemed to lead into a future
paved entirely in blackness, coal.

A scattering of stars, a slice of Moon,
the prick of a pink planet, Mars, I think,
took pity on me, like the passing cars.
Those headlights allowed me to pick out
a discarded pack of Camels which
concealed one cigarette and puff of air.
How incredible that find: how Moon
and Mars, Camel and cars, kept
me company that night. But the sparks

of a tossed Marlboro let me smoke
where I was going—a dim, orange glow.

I thanked the driver as he sped away,
truck dwindling to a pair of rubies. I
had no matches in my pocket—no-
thing useful, no money, no house keys:
a Latin book in my backpack, Ovid's
Metamorphoses, toothbrush, clothes,
socks and soiled underwear. And still
how lucky I felt—and not too cold—
now that I could smoke. The poetry
we'd write together was so far away—
farther than Mars, that truck driver, you

standing naked in L.A. And love,
while that Camel lasted, didn't seem
a possibility all that remote.

Breaking the Camel's Back

Camels and Michelob—from white trash cowboy to
white collar slave; *ooo*, I have such finer things
planned for you! Asheville brew, Scottish booze; a
fag to puff on that perpetually glows—and a butt that
won't stop smoking ...

And all I ask is your pure, unadulterated addiction.

*   *   *   *   *

BTW, I would have picked you up that night, on that
lone dark highway-to-Metamorphosis; I wouldn't have
let you smoke, but I would have taken you home and
made you forget your religion, your mom and dad and
all things bad ...

The Road to Hell is just the backdoor to Heaven.

*   *   *   *   *

We are winged creatures from another world, you and
I and "our kind," moons that wobble between the
globes and leave no calculable orbit; every eviction is an
invitation, every assassination an ascension, where we
alight, poems are written ...

We who delight in crime!

Damascus

Yes, pick me up, dust me off, fill
my mouth with testicles, goat-cheese, grapes,
change my oil, enlarge my cock, replace
my heart with something softer than the plum
stone I suspect is throbbing there. Be
Prometheus to me, be Frankenstein, but leave
the memory of that lonely road intact.
I wasn't ready then—to hold a pen
or penis properly. Forget a hand.
There is this transformation I still have
to undergo, to be myself. I smoked

that solitary Camel to Damascus.
The butt the truck driver flung from his cab
seemed a sign—a well-meant meteor
crashing against the asphalt, splashing sparks,
rolling to a stop ten feet away,
glowing. I ran to pick it up, before
the filthy filter put the fire out! I had
no matches, maybe, but I had a chance
to put one corner of my Cosmos right,
light the lost cigarette I found—to
let my lungs fill up with poetry.

To accept the universe like this,
to welcome an old Camel as just one
of those small gifts that Providence bestows,
is harder for me now than it was then.
I'm older and less flexible. I've lost
some of my looks, the hair I once dyed red,
my combat boots, the 1950s trench
I pawned my silver boom box for—
all those external things I thought were me—
adorn a boy I fear is dead. His ghost

appears in steamy windows. He haunts
my eyes when I am shaving. When I fuck,
I make the love he was incapable of
making. I do this in his memory.
I regard tattoos and scars the way
he looked at certain birthdays. Something must
remain besides the pools of melting ice
cream and wax. Still pictures. Poetry.
All we carry over from the past.
Stale Camels. Cars. A butt flung from a truck
rolling to a stop somewhere. Like here.

Happy Samhain, Darling,

Goddess knows I've done my share of making love to
ghosts—West Hollywood cadavers, San Francisco
zombies, 8th Avenue ephemera of the sordid kind—but
I was stumbling then, I hadn't lost God; I was still
fumbling around in someone else's delusion. Then

in some etheric closet I perceived the Light, a
door cracked, a way to escape—and I made a
run for it! Darkness turned to Light, Dorothy Parker to
Hafiz, "making love" to *being* Love; this time when the
train left the station I was at the wheel; and the

goblin took wing, took song, and became the
Lark of Spring.

This week I had implanted my first bionic tooth—a
titanium screw into my lower mandible; I have
felt no pain, the process clean, the surgeon a
hottie; I cannot wait to bite something! You are
dear to me, as you are *now;* and at 55 I feel

prepared to make young love to you—younger
love than ever I could before; for I have been made
anew—no Frankenstein's monster from borrowed
parts, from someone else's closet—a babe in the
woods, frightened not at all, but

joyous of his own inherent Nature.

So let the boogiemen swarm and storm—Repub-
licans, Christians, the homo elite … they cannot
touch us for we are Divine; angels feather our
nest, and the Tree that holds us grows steadily up-
ward toward Galaxy Center.

Ah men.

Sanctuary

Today I had my first full kiss with a donkey—named
Lehua; Lehua won't accept a cheek or a forehead—tho she
did nibble on my chin-scruff for a time—she likes it
lip-to-lip (and she is not slim in the lip department); a
sleek and bespeckled Chinese deer named

Veronica was less aggressive, but no less nuzzly, and
tagged me like a dog for an hour; Morpheus, a young
obsidian-cloaked billy, just wanted to be cradled and carried a-
round everywhere I went; even the 100-some roosters and
hens were vying to be held and scratched about the

ear feathers. Not so friendly was Moby the pig, both
blind and deaf from a childhood of abuse; still, I've never
been to a farm quite like it—tomorrow I begin con-
struction of a grandiose rabbit pen and warren, which my
Alice, Benjamin and Beatrix will move into. I

like a man what eats what I feeds him, enjoys a good
scratchin' behind the ears, and shits when and where he
damn well pleases; I like a man what rolls over for
special treats and stays within earshot on a mountain
trail; I like a man what nibbles my beard and

knows where the sleepin' is good.

Animal Sanctuary

I'm sure your rabbits will be happy there.
Yours sound much friendlier than mine—
that asylum I was once placed in—
church: a clean, cadaverous Baptist
interior, supported by dark ribs,
a space capable of accommodating
a thousand souls according to the Fire
Department restrictions. Our crazy
choir sang hymns in satin pajamas, blue,
piano on the left, organ on the right,
a madman in the middle. I would poke
holes in his upholstery with a pencil
I sharpened for that specific purpose.
I longed for an Apocalypse—a really
loud fart—a nuclear catastrophe—
a final trumpet—to put an end to
the announcements—trustees meetings, deaths—
Epistles to the Galatians, Colossians,
Galoshes, Dalmatians, and the wrinkly
sound of hands, in unison, just
flipping pages. It went on forever.
The Lord's Supper proved such a meager
meal, hardly even a snack, really—
matzo fragments and a thimble of Welch's
grape juice—I was forbidden. (I was
never baptized.) I wanted to
get out, go to McDonald's, anywhere,
for lunch. I poked the pew impatiently,
I drew a zillion pairs of Golden Arches—
MMMMMM—in the back of my Bible—
filling up the white end pages—those
God left blank after Revelation. I
loved the hymns. I loathed the sermons. They
ended with Amens at one, with my

stomach angrily growling. That's why
I am so glad you're adding your own
ecclesiastical flair to that Maui
sanctuary. I bet communion in
any safe haven you would devise
would keep demented parsons out, but still
admit a few strange boys in bunny suits—
those looking to gnaw on a raw carrot,
or thirsty for some unusual tipple,
you would smile and generously provide.

Catechism

Church was the first place I ever got diddled with, I'm
rather grateful to it for that—way cooler than my
 suck-shit Catholic school; Protestants diddle among them-
selves—no priest required. I spent today digging and
 planting postholes and posts for what will be a

most fine rabbit domain, assisted by five bunnies, two
donkeys, Veronica the deer, nine very helpful goats, and
 more chickens and ducks than I could count; church is a
poor substitute for nature—which is why the saints of the
 world often end up in caves, woods, or hoeing

cabbage in some meager village. I like dressed-up old
ladies, I really do—when they're not all crippled with
 bigotry and hate—but I received more kisses today (of
the cloven kind) than I have ever received from even the
 most inspired congregation. And then home to seven

kitties, thrumming their paws, wondering where I had
been all day, and about those strange and exotic phero-
 mones all over my sleeves and pant legs. So it's
nature not "hate your"; it's catechism not cata-
 clysm; exhaustion not boredom; and the hymns of

bamboo branches clacking in the coming squall, and
gutter spouts drumming on the gingers and taro, that
 let me know that all is right with my world, that
Goddess is present and abounding, and that Love ex-
 ists in more furry places than I will ever have

 time for.
(I look forward to the day when you, too, kneel
 down and nibble from my hand; we
fuck like bunnies, and
 nap upon a bed of fresh-laid hay …).

Dur et Corné

My Dear, it's hard to write, the Mèniére's disease and the
gins-and-Limonata are making my eyes swim; my fingers are
 blurry, and even the fawning spell check seems vague and
uncertain. You are passed out in a basement in Connecti-
cut (I know that that's a state, but I cannot place it) a

bottle of bourbon up your ass; it really is cruel that
you're a drunken slut without me—and me cuckolded by a
 tawdry fifth—I would so enjoy using your lack of
equilibrium to my advantage! Life is bothersome and the
 miles in between us a bore; and so I count the

days (clichéd tho it may be) until I wear your sphincter like a
ring of engagement and fall asleep to your gurgling in my
pillow. This is poem #2 today—for want of a response to
the last—I am sorry poetry is not as effortless to
 you as it is to me; I am sorry your work is

tedious and time-consuming, your 110 bosses annoying, and
that the wheels of the Big Grapple rattle your windows as
 they churn pointlessly by—you know I have little patience for
society's vainglorious Sturm und Drang. But there we
 have it, drunk and swooning on two different

sides of the earth, oceans mountains rivers between
us, a bottle of bourbon and a bottle of gin standing in for the
 flesh that seeks its counter and the spirit that longs to
see itself reflected in the eyes and heart and smile of a-
 nother soldier of Eternity's inebriated perfection; piss-

hard and horny, la tua capra onesti, il Gav

Commuter Blues

Leaning against a leaky lav—
this morning on the 8:04
express, hurtling toward another
day in New York, I read the piece

you sent last night. I felt so sad.
The sun seemed bright and pointless—
a single knitting needle stuck in
a gigantic ball of orange yarn.

I've nothing to look forward to—
there's nothing on my schedule—
except the poem I will write
for you. I'm always happy to

write poems. But I'm afraid
Art is no substitute for life.
No matter what I say, or do,
that happy feeling never lasts.

I Want to Be the Bottle You Get Drunk With

Today I mixed concrete and set the posts for the two
chain-link gates leading into *Mundus Cuniculi* and out
again into the pasture at large; swarms of goats proffered
their sincere assistance by both making hoofprints in the
fresh crete, and in nibbling my beard whenever my

posture permitted. The hardest work is now complete, the
remainder will be creative fun with fencing, warren-
construction, and of course bunny landscaping; and then my dear
conies' paws touch the earth and their lives are their
own at last. I cannot wait for you to

experience the farm; I think it will be as easy and
natural for you as peeing in a hot bath, or the first time we
do the deed. Thursday week we touchdown and slide in-
to each others' lives and colons; my writing partner's an alco-
holic, so there will be plenty of

lubrication; and you will get to see San Francisco for the
very first time (… it's like *so* 1987!), meet my
brother, and munch your fill on my dangling parti-
ciples. I am not the sort of rancher what trims his billy's
horns—in fact I plan to hang onto them when I

take you out for a ride; but the truth be told, I
do plan to keep you on a tight tether, daemon, and
milk you for every metaphor you're worth!

> *I want to be the bottle you get drunk with,*
> *I want to be the cellmate you get punked by,*
> *I want to be the sistah you get funked with,*
> *I want to ride your broom into the sky;*

You make my alethiometer shudder,

> —*Caper Deus Tuus, Pan*

Mundus Cuniculi

Of all your incarnations—
from growling Siva to
pipe blowing Pan,
to Miss Emily Dick-
inson, who borrows your
mouth, occasionally,
whispering suggestions
into my pink, erect
blushingly sensitive
rabbit ears—this curious
blend of personae—
Adam and Hadrian—
animal man and Roman
emperor—suits
your affections best.

No fig leaves for you,
no Eden either, now
painfully aware how
booby-trapped apples
tend to explode.
You mind your mattock,
count your chickens,
look after your goats,
having learned the hard
way about gardens:
you acknowledge your
past, then bathe
your ass. Paradise—
you have other things—
other concerns. Like Eve,

you are a busy man.
you have concrete

to pour—a *Mundus*
Cuniculi—a Bunny
World to build—
a legacy to leave
behind for all
the furry creatures
who have been nursed
in your lap, called
your pubic bone
a home. I think
when you depart this
volcanic island
sanctuary, Maui, for

the life hereafter, Black
Mountain, North
Carolina, no one
will feel abandoned by
an absconded God
goofing off in Asheville.
Bunny World will
remain: evidence a
few emperors exist
besides Caligula.
I bet, in the future,
small mammals will regard
your works with wonder, like
lost hikers do the wall
of Hadrian—who,
you know, was gay.

Pan-demonium

Were you my little goat, I would keep you in a
controlled but vast pasture; green green green, and
all the clover you could eat. You would sleep with
me and nibble on my toes at night; I would
coddle you like Jesus holds his lamb, or over

my shoulder like Francis with his sparrow. No
more Upper East Side wolves salivating on your
chops, no more dogshit between your cloves or
garbage in your snout; your golden eyes would
be the best of my morning and an in-

vitation to a pre-brunch wrestle, my hands
firmly on your horns. Knowing goats as I do, your
hooves on my back would be more of a
romp than a challenge; you seek the high
places that few men have straddled ... too

few, I must say. So flick your tail, my friend, and
know that you have already won; lead me into
verdant pastures and let's have this out, beard to
beard, man to nature, wild upon wild, where
only the hornéd may travel.

The Lay Of The Land

However the topography turns out—
how green the grass, how succulent the clover,
the types of trees, the quantity of shade,
how the branches vary through the seasons,

through all weathers, fair or foul, if clouds
define the upper boundaries of the place,
or if a sprinkling of thistles, stars, forms
the borders we bump up against—I know

these features, fences, all those limits
amount to nothing—one of those jokes
time and space make at our expense.
I feel your arms enfolding me, like Freddy,

the bright black billy in your photograph.
The area inside your heart is infinite
according to our calculations. We are
no ordinary goats. We've done the math.

A Mid-autumn Morning's Pastorale

Today, on Maui, we are in the midst of our first
winter storm—mainlanders would laugh at what
we call a winter storm, but *we* know that it's
happening; I won't be able to get much done at the
sanctuary—but can adjust my gates, take some

measurements for the hutch, and spread some
carrots and sweet potatoes around; I will spend
more time at the gym, and coconut-curry soup at
the hunky-hippy wagon after. In another re-
ality, far far away, I am sitting in a farm-

house in Black Mountain, NC, organizing my
pot roast or lamb stew, while the chilly rains
bounce and cavort against the panes; by the ever-
blazing fire sits a hobbit, his face in a collection of
Elizabeth Bishop, hirsute hobbit toes pointed at the

flames, two plumped testicles rising and falling in
the heat like dumplings bobbling on a fine *tarte
faisan*. Cats abound on poofs and stools and piles of
books, licking their own savory regions; Anton
Bruckner in the background (perhaps the

9th). He has put down his book and parted my
legs, while the stew gently roils and the rain to
our first silent snow. (There is nothing hobbits a-
dore more than parsnips; perhaps for tomorrow a
proper shepherd's pie ....)

Satyriasis

I have slimmed down a bit—tho not as much as
hoped—for our first encounter, but more for our
  reading in the city; it's been a while since I've been
naked for the public, and a while since I've been
  naked for a man at all. Of course, who wants to get

  fucked by a man who looks like he lives off of
celery sticks, shaves his legs and spends his evenings
  on the aerobic machines at the gym; give me a man with
mud on his boots and teeth-marks on his arms, a beard that
  wants trimming and toenails that draw blood, sadness in his

  voice and wisdom in his eyes. I know you will
love me as I am; scars bring metaphors to the table, the
  memories of dead lovers have been replaced by godly
incantations in ink; and I smell now of wood and
  fecund earth. My antlers have an edge of

  blood. Vegans are appetizers, not a main course; cars
are designed for crashing; one can never make one's
  chai too sweet; making a living is of no concern of the
Poet. We are ephemera, chimeras of the night; cho-
  lesterol and blood pressure are the fancies of

  sissies and secretaries, wusses and lawyers, agents,
salesmen and hucksters; piss cures everything. I
  want to sleep with you beneath celestial displays while
coyotes encircle in ceremony and song; I give you
  snakes and venom, badgers and polecats ... and a

word of advice: *Don't think twice!* Let blood be our
mixer, semen our sustenance, let the heavens erase all
 timidity of soul; I embrace you thru Siva's
ashes, love you thru Krsna's dance, and sanctify you on the
 holy cross. May the sacred crows of the field

pick clean our shining bones!

Ragoût de Hobbit

Goddess knows my cooking instincts are brilliant! (Did
you know that about me?) I cheffed a great rainy-night
stew tonight; caramelizing onions and carrots in ghee made a
wonderful sweet base, along with both coconut and
cow cream; burger, shiitake, Italian parsley and

kale rounded out the body; sundried tomatoes and a
half bottle of bad pumpkin beer gave it brightness and
sour. You will not want for flavor of a rainy winter's
night; I was a pastry chef for years in WeHo; I've
cooked for movie stars, billionaires and yogic

masters. All I need's a fire, a long wooden table (a
stump will do in a pinch) and a hungry hobbit to
cook for. No skinny chicken breasts here, my food
oozes and dribbles down hairy chins; flavors
linger of the chest for rumination. The

question is: If I garden the food, I chop and I
dice, an ounce of my spit and the sweat from my
brow … will you, would you, eat from my bowl? curl
up at my feet with your paws in the air, and
allow me to lick clean your whiskers?

Second Thoughts

I admit, I had them. Second thoughts.
You said that Verlaine and Rimbaud might be
the sort of partnership we could explore
poetically. I groaned inside, "Here we go—
how boring, how predictable, no way—
how un-American. He wants to waste
my time, my tears and sweat, reviving such
a precious pair of little dickheads." No thanks.
I walked through the East Village eyeing others—
mostly chicks. That sad relationship
would never do: a lousy metaphor
Verlaine/Rimbaud—a vacant stretch of earth
so intensely alkali even
the few rocks living there all want to die.

A dizzy spell, a rest, a little chai,
you stirred around with a tattoo. The gym,
the sight of Omar's smooth Brazilian glans—
peeping at my firm, white fanny through
his loose foreskin—tantalized my teeth.
You gave the problem of our partnership
a bit more thought. Americans we'd be:
Emily and Edna, Dickinson, Millay,
wild words for you, soiled sainthood for me.
You made an offer I could not refuse.
I got to travel to Kyoto and
sleep in cherry blossoms, study monks,
write imaginary letters to a friend
laid up with Ménière's disease.

Since returning from Japan, you have
been many things to me besides dizzy,
Emily: Diane Arbus, Siva, Gandalf,
goats top the list of your identities;

you are a martyr to Satyriasis,
Antonius's lover, Hadrian,
the Emperor of Bunny World. What
you have not been with me so far,
sweetheart, is vulnerable to harm.
Nor will you be that man until next week,
when we finally meet. Jet-lagged, sand-bagged,
you will learn with horror I am not
quite the gal you ordered—not at all.
I am Cleopatra. I studied art

under Julius Caesar: how the heart
divides in parts. I march through men like Gaul.

If You Meet the Gav on the Road ...

Who are we ever but fictions that yearn to
break free, equines that desire control of their
own tether, golems in search of a soul ... *Gavin
Dillard,* you say? I googled him once and came
up with 133,000 entries!—I read an article about

how Gavin gave Rock Hudson the dreaded
AIDS that eventually killed him (tho I personally
have no recollection of meeting the man); we are
poets, you and I, and as much creatures of fiction as
descriers of Truth. So,

if you meet Gavin Dillard on the road, as the
Buddhists would say, kill him. If you meet him in
bed, love him—and give him my love as well;
I'll keep writing poems about us and following
the story. And when at

last you're deep inside the man, and he in-
side of you, that Presence that you feel there,
that Light, as it were, will be none other than
you—no no, not the Eric Thomas Norris we all
pretend to know and love, but the

Truth of Who we Are, Now and Forever,
        Amen.

Mosquitoes

You burned all your wood last night, you say.
Let's see if I have anything you can
haul back to Maui for those wretched nights—
when you're hemmed in by darkness, pouring rain,
trapped in the tropics, slapping phantoms, those
mosquitoes sucking all your blood away.

I'll look around New York, see what I have:
a coffee table, couch, bed, some books—
mostly memorized. My life is yours,
if you can carry it. Chop it up. Stick
it in your hearth, or build a fire out back—
invite the insects to enjoy the blaze.

None of my possessions make sense anymore
except as kindling. What good are books
in bed—even yours? All I want is you.
Poems might as well be mosquitoes for all
the joy they give. Burn them. Burn everything.
Fuck everything. Let's go somewhere else and live.

The Tao of Gav

After 30-some years of spotty discipleship, I have
ended up #1 student, awake and realized, of my
 original and God-given Gurus; during which time I
sat with, cooked for, hung-out-backstage-with half the
 famous teachers of the millennium. After a period of

disenfranchisement—self-inflicted—I needled and
cajoled by way back into good graces, giving up all
 other search and eventually *all* search, and accepting the
final verdict—that there is nothing to get and no
 one to get it. Which means all that spiritual

seeking is over—*fait accompli*—which means I am
free to be who I am without question or pause; which
does *not* mean I don't get lonely or bored or angry or
drunk-and-stupid (as some erroneously informed con-
 temporary hacks may claim); it does mean that I will

no longer need to incarnate into 3D (tho Guruji says
that I will opt to one last time). Animals love me even
 more than ever because I am ever more present; homo-
sexuals avoid me more than ever because they can't
 perceive my agenda; children love me more than

I wish they did. And when I cook now I really
cook, when I write I rarely think or stumble, when I
 garden you may not see me until the stars come
out; and when I make love … well, it's been too
 long to know about that! But I can tell you

this, mister, for I know it in my heart, that
when you have me prone before you,
 like so much squealing pork, you'll
know I have no agenda but the
 pleasure of your fork.

No Agenda

I've never asked for an agenda, dear,
only you—content to follow where
a moment leads: another moment, Mars,
an elephant tattoo, a rabbit hutch,
mosquitoes, Maui, mountains, sex,

love plain and simple. Still, I must confess,
each poem I compose for you, I die
a bit in writing—mingling my dust
with yours. There might be better ways to spend
my afternoons. But not eternity.

Nuts and Berries

Somewhere, in a cabin in the woods, two animals of
very different stripes sprawl in front of a dwindling
fire; their spent passion has turned to grooming—they
lick each other's paws and cheeks. They were not
meant to come together—they are from very

different forests—but the storm brought them to this
sanctuary; they made love because they *could*, because
it was right. Tonight they will sleep inside each
other's dreams, the scent of their fur lingering in the
fire's sunset glow, tails overlapped, their

snouts against one another. Tonight the storm will
blow and they will be close—closer than ever they
have been to another; the occasional growl or
show of fangs is but a teaser. And tomorrow, when the
gale has passed and the sun come out,

who knows what berries they might pick together?

Aunties and Uncles (Honoring One's Aumakua)

We are the children of Catullus, you and I, offspring of
Socrates and Sappho, Khristós and Dionysos, Shikibu and
 Basho, Blake, Whitman, Isherwood and Crisp, Nina
Simone, Buffy Sainte-Marie, Janis, Morrissey and
 Wham! Poetry is our conversation, our transformation, our

 consummation; we have been frightened and enlightened, for-
saken and awakened, sanctified and southern-fried; we are a
 tome-in-the-making. Tolstoy and Tolkien were uncles, you
see, T H White an evil auntie; The Lady Chablis the mummy we
never had, Nijinsky the snake in our panties. Martha

Graham choreographed this, Mae West penned quips for our
nuptials; Mishima died for our sins; for we, my be-
loved, are the harbingers of bliss—for Freedom exists in every
first kiss—a cavalcade of Saints await agog. My point being, in
all of this, is that were we not to come together, make

 cosmic love—fuck like ninjas—we would be dis-
appointing, dishonoring, disillusioning, an awful lot of
 Thems what Paved the Way.

Legacy

"But now the suitors trooped in with all their swagger
And took their seats on low and high backed chairs."

— Homer, The Odyssey, I.169-170., tr. Robert Fagles

Since one should never grant Reality
jurisdiction over human life,
I've been rewriting Homer's *Odyssey*—
pretending I'm Ulysses. You're my wife
in this new version, my Penelope.
I come—exhausted—from the arms of strife:
I've just spent seven years inside a cave,
the plaything of Calypso. A love slave

is not the life for me. Though divine,
love making's rather hard upon the knees
when you're my age. And men must watch their wine
if working with large machinery. Please,
Penelope, be patient. I'll be fine.
A lifetime of adventures on rough seas
can leave a sailor—no—I won't say limp—
but—for seven years I lived on shrimp,

oysters, clams, and lobster thermidor—
foods rich in zinc—a bitter chemical.
I don't know what the oysters use it for.
I merely note that zinc's available
in several things I don't eat anymore.
Calypso used it for cholesterol:
she liked to think of me as her dessert
and careful preparation couldn't hurt.

Calypso's kitchen—her exotic flair
with spices, strange devices, and romance—
left me, most mornings, paralyzed, I fear.
I don't think love stood much of a chance
between us. No. Nymphs do not declare
affection for a pair of underpants
kept folded in a drawer for twenty years.
And nymphs do not dissolve, like salt, in tears.

Come here, Penelope. Have some champagne.
This crystal's a great improvement on the shoe
I used to drink from. I am so ashamed.
The things that cruel Calypso made me do—
every word she uttered was profane.
She was a scorpion, compared to you,
my dear—Penelope—my darling wife.
I'm lucky I escaped her with my life.

Penelope, I've something to discuss.
I have been thinking of retirement—
abandoning the hot, Homeric fuss
for an existence less—well—violent:
to be a janitor, to drive a bus—
pay taxes, and the butcher, and the rent!
Shall I say, "Sayonara," to the port,
and take up bowling, or some other sport?

I know a few objections might be raised.
Ulysses may show up in Babylon,
in jokes, immortalized as the milkmaid
who is discovered in a leather thong
behind a big bull, spying. I have prayed
for guidance from the gods—prayed hard and long—
and Heaven has been silent. I am still
Ulysses—King of Ithaca. I will

not live forever. Yes, much earlier,
we should have had this little conversation.
In retrospect, too much may be too clear
to men involved in the affairs of any nation ...

wasn't Telemachus's hair much curlier,
and lighter, when I left? He's changed. Our son.
Not only taller. He smiles like a stone.
How does he handle sitting on my throne?

Would you consider the lad self-reliant?
Do dingy diplomats command his ear?
"Son, listen, nobody could blind a giant—
a brute like Polyphemus—with a spear—
forget a charred broomstick. All the science
indicates he'd die." I want to hear
about our boy, dear. Tell me, did he sigh
with satisfaction when he learnt I didn't die?

He has this distant look that bothers me:
as if his dad were a museum piece—
an amphora—a piece of pottery
dredged up from somewhere after centuries.
Does he realize he's won the lottery?
I am Ulysses—not some fool with fleas
you try to pity, briefly, till the smells
begin to catch up with your nostrils.

Perhaps we should have named the child Mike ...
Are you certain that he belongs to us?
When I left Ithaca, he was a tyke—
so tiny. You raised him yourself. I trust
your judgment, dear—your motherly insight.
Would he object to being devious
in a world where honest men cannot be found?
Please tell me that he walks on solid ground.

I want to know what kind of man he is,
Penelope, because, when we are dead,
this palace—and our people—will be his.
Us, this antique furniture—the bed
where you received a young man with a kiss
that shook the stars—or so the servants said—
might easily be tossed into the fire
and not be missed. And I would be a liar

if I said otherwise. Penelope—
I'm old. I'm tired. I'm dying for a bath.
I'd settle for a pot in which to pee.
Penelope, downstairs, they'll hear you laugh!
You haven't changed. You're still my Queen, I see.
I never doubted you. But when I asked
about Telemachus your face turned white—
as if you'd seen a ghost. He'll be all right.

Though in the banquet hall, as I speak, great
cups of wine are being passed around,
as fifty pairs of lips prepare to break
fresh bread together. I can hear the sound
as fifty greedy mouths agree to take
turns with you, my dear, Ithaca's crown.
For twenty years, they've gorged themselves at will:
tomorrow I present them with the bill.

I didn't travel all the way from Troy
to just roll over, like a dog, and die.
I won't let any harm befall our boy—
but something must be done. Let him try,
Penelope. The gods do not destroy
these parasites. Telemachus and I
do that. He says he's gay. I'm glad he's Greek.
The gods gave him your heart and my physique.

Orpheus Ascending

"To Zeus Astrapaios (Lightning Maker). I call the mighty, holy, splendid, light, aerial, dreadful-sounding, fiery-bright, flaming, ethereal light, with angry voice, lighting through lucid clouds with crashing noise. Untamed, to whom resentments dire belong, pure, holy power, all-parent, great and strong: come, and benevolent these rites attend, and grant the mortal life a pleasing end."

— Orphic Hymn 20 to Lightning Zeus

I don't love the poem, dear; it reverts back to being
clever. Okay, I like the poem, but it adds nothing to our
 dialog; and in four days I don't want to fuck your
clever. I'd rather see you cry than be erudite; I want an
 open heart and trembling emotions. I want us

 terrified and fragile, like Grandma's Russian
crystal, too frail to unpack, too beautiful not to dis-
 play. I bought condoms tonight—*Lambskins*—oh I
know they're not politically correct, but they
 remind me of nights on Crete, our hooves in a

 frenzy of clacking; they make me want to pull
grapes from your anus. I bought several oils and
 lotions from Whole Foods—in less-than-four-
ounce containers; I have chocolates and Cialis, a
 manuscript, and hosts of seraphim well-

 wishers (or onlookers, as the case may be); I have
kisses that are burning within my cheeks. I don't
 care if you burst into tears or into laughter, as
long as you melt within my arms; I want you too
 flustered to be clever. It is not that I don't

admire your brain—as I said in the beginning, I
love that you are smarter than me; I can use a
walking calculator and reference guide!—but I
plan to keep my finger always upon the On/Off
switch. I plan to show you content you have

yet to calculate, and mythologies thus far beyond
your ken; I plan to use you up, and then breathe
life back into your fragile human clay; by the fire-
god Agni, and master smythe Hephaestus, shall my
dorje find its mark, and leave us both

spent beyond mortal comprehension!

Ulysses and Penelope

Scared? Don't make me laugh. Seized from
behind, I once felt the barrel of a gun
pressed against my skull by a big thug
hissing in my ear, "I'm gonna blow
your fucking brains out!" I sassed the ass-
hole back, "At least, I've got some brains to
blow out." Moron. I admit I'm stuck

three days before we're scheduled to meet,
a little nervous, yes, reluctant to
be so fresh with you. To stand naked
in front of a strange crowd is easier
than exposing the sharp edges of my
New York tongue to a monk and mystic
starry-eyed as California. Well,

Ulysses and Penelope, maybe
I was wrong to look at us this way—
as human beings, not the things we are:
demigods, a race apart. Although
it kills me to admit mistakes, so
be it. In San Francisco, I shall see
we only commit bestiality.

Field Notes on a Courtship

*"You make my man parts rage, and my
lady parts quiver..."*

— Gavid's Megamorphoses

1.
I love you. So fuck off.

2.
Hi, my name is Gavin. I am older than you, taller than you, more
experienced and published than you; I am part Mongol and have
many more tattoos than you. I'm looking for a worthy disciple;
call me @ 808/LUV-JUNK

3.
I want you raw over ice. Hold the wasabi—I've got my own.

4.
I have lost ten pounds since we began this tome. What that
means for you is that, in the likely event that you go down on
me, you will not be suffocated by my jiggling belly; what it means for
me is that I will be able to enjoy watching without impediment the
contortions of your mouth.

5.
I have become proficient in the plow pose; what that means for both
of us is that I can watch you lunch on my ass.

6.
If I had been there, and held the gun, no way you would have
escaped!

7.
I want you naked on a city street, in the rain, as angry crowds
taunt us, threaten, and hurl obscenities.

8.
I'm all about myths; let's create a whopper.

9.
Having lost ten pounds in six weeks, my ass feels a bit de-
flated. It may take a couple more months to adjust and "snap back";
I'll bring gaffer's tape.

10.
In two days I'm going to pick you up and drink your saliva like
my life depended upon it.

11.
I plan to sleep—if and when I sleep—with your
prostate beneath my pillow.

Revenge

I am learning how to bleed
without clotting. To be myself,
in other words, submit to what
my heart is telling me. You are
the most irritating prick I've
never met. You won't stop poking
your nose in my most private parts.
You should be crucified. You

ask for blood. Well, here it is,
just leave my veins running in-
definitely. I won't run out.
I must love you, because you bring
no peace of mind, no solace, no-
thing, but insomnia and
strange fevers at odd hours. God
damn your appetite. Your mouth.

This is what I look forward to.
Torment. Waking up at 4:00
AM, checking my e-mail
to see if you have written. No.
You shit and trample on my dreams
even when you say nice things.
Absurd. You—you sleep peacefully
a million miles away. That is

not fair. That is not fair at all.
So I am sending a cloud of
mosquitoes to drive you mad.
A few may have malaria,
so you had better smack the right ones.
They will be there, biting you,
forever buzzing in your ears.
So you can feel what I feel. Now.

And You Can Kiss My Kismet

Yeah, well, fuck you too, up one side and down the
other—head in the toilet and ass in my nostrils—scream for
me, bitch, and call my name like you mean it! I take your
challenge, from midnight until morn, cum'on give it
to me, my balls are aimed and loaded. Inquiring

readers want to know: Does he love me yet? Is he
moist and fragrant? You see, the readers won't get to be a
part of our consummation; so you can pout all you
want about technique and story arcs, but the time for
metaphor has passed—it's time to

give the reader what s/he paid for, what s/he's been
waiting for. I made love this afternoon to nine goats, two
burros, a deer, and a large Silver Rex coney named
Ethan; I never saw who stole my hat. Today we made a
counter-offer to the Swiss folk who want to

buy the Maui house—I'm certain they're going to
accept it; if all plays out the way it seems, we'll be in
Black Mountain for Thanksgiving—dinner with the
Gurus—buy our farm, and be moved and settled by
2011. So you see, it's time to drink the Stuff of

Life, to give the finger to Mommy and Daddy and
plunge into that rabbit hole; I won't disappoint you, or
drop you, I have Blake on one arm, Lao Tzu on the other, and a
hard-on the size of Manhattan. But above all I have
trust in God, and know when my boy's

ripe for a spanking.

Porn and Poetry

Our audience, I think, could not care less
if I love you, as long as we have sex
at some stage in this book. I suggest
a public consummation best performed
in San Francisco, New York, or Berlin—
unless the Vatican's available—some
great city frothy with hot spunk and piss,
the gay equivalents of milk and honey.

I'm proud to say I've never disappointed
a paying customer in my entire
life. I'm always glad to grab my shins—
to cackle, squeal, or bray—imitate
the perfect piglet, chicken, or wild donkey
the poor things dream of boning in the dark.
I know what readers want. Pornography
enjoys a wider base of fans than love.

Game Point

Have you cold feet, my child? I will warm them;
cold emotions? I will storm them; Love is
neither beast nor heroic feat; indeed, it is the
least common denominator. And even the cynical-est, most
frost-bit old faggots crave Love.

BTW, what's this I hear about you being an Olympic-class
badminton champion? (I must remember to watch my
birdies closely!) There is so much we have to
learn about one another—I look forward to inciting your
backhand ...

*   *   *   *   *

I hate it when you're asleep and I'm not. It's brutal, un-
fair; I can hear your soft breathing from here. At least when I
move back to WeNoCa we'll be in the same time zone—I can
chide and harass you twice the hours, ploy for good-
night kisses, and know that when I'm having my morning

chai, you are just recently coffeed-up. It's not a snout be-
tween my legs, but it's certainly some small thing, I should
think. But tomorrow we land in a median time zone; you will
be three-hours more tired than I, you can try to sleep while I
poke around in your privates. (Good luck with that.)

*   *   *   *   *

As for the kitties, bunnies, goats and chickens, I leave
them yams, alfalfa, gobo and all good things; they shall not
 want (and have Uncle Noah to fend for them). I come for a
different beast, one I will trap in my arms and squeeze un-
 til he squeals, a staturally impaired biped with a

wit that can rend flesh and legs that can surely outrun a
flabby old mule like me—but not to worry, as I know to
 keep a cinched grip; I am bringing dark chocolates and
Irish spirits, and a will used to taming even the
 brokenest of wild things.

*   *   *   *   *

And so my noetic ninja, my nubile nemesis, nefarious
nubbins, we meet at last;
 I beg thee, tempestuous tyrant, tenacious tuchus, lascivious
Lilliputian, have mercy on this decrepit, agéd monk, who
 seeks but to salivate at thy holy feet!

O secretious shave-pate, I lick your belly for good luck and
guzzle of thy healing waters,
 O effluvial elf, for tho unworthy, you will find me your most
fawning faun and salacious servant; from the first thrust-and-
parry you had already won!

Your supine supplicant awaits with open loins and
mind, may the universe be our eternal bed, your colon my
 sheath and my comfort, as it is from the first
rimming, now and 'til the
 end of rhyme.

 Om Eric Om Thomas Om Norris!

The End of Rhyme

I do not have cold feet. I am afraid,
when this is finished, I will have to find
something else to do besides write
chatty letters and bad poetry.

As much as coffee, your e-mails have
become a part of my morning routine.
How should I wake up to a blank screen—
nothing from Gavin Dillard? I mean,

we close this book, one chapter of our lives,
begin another one tonight, in flesh,
fresh ink, fresh paper, new possibilities.
The words we've written will remain. But

what will they mean to us tomorrow, when
we wake up in San Francisco? Will
we leave behind those separate lives
we lived before? How will we appear

to one another in the morning? How
much older, fatter, or more frail,
a thousand years from now? I hope we'll be
associated then, at least on paper,

less with art, than a belief in love.
Though Maui and New York, 6000 miles,
age, HIV, experience, different
styles of writing and sleep schedules

might have concluded things another way,
before we found a publisher: you
and I found Bryan. Here we go then. Down.
I must put my laptop away. It seems

we've started our descent for Oakland.
I will be holding you in a few hours.
Meanwhile, I plan to close my eyes and pray
we both land safely. What else can I say?

Love is a Poem

Love is a misnomer, for it implies duality, purports
two disparate parts intertwined; but it is the
 best concept we have that can be expressed in a
word. It is bigger than, but inclusive of the
 notion that I want to die inside your

 colon—which erroneously suggests an "I," a
colon, or death as an actuality; but we
 know better, you and I, for we are One and
merely experiencing a coming-together, a re-
 union, an epiphany—which is bigger than, but

 inclusive of the fact that I want to fuck you six
ways before we first settle in to sleep to-
 gether, to breathe for a night—for four nights—the
same bepassioned air. And if you
 do not already know it, young poet, then trust my

 words, that I am with you now and will never be
apart from you—which is bigger than, but
 inclusive of the fact that I demand unlimited
access—or at least first rights-of-refusal—to your
 deepest recesses, and the

Precious Child that we have begot.

*   *   *   *   *

Love is a poem; let us, my friend,
be the right choice of words.

— A Man

❦

About the Poets

Gavin Geoffrey Dillard has published ten collections of verse, two anthologies, and his infamous Hollywood tell-all, *IN THE FLESH: Undressing for Success*. Also known as "The Naked Poet," his poems have been recorded by James Earl Jones, Don Adams, and published in anthologies and periodicals worldwide. The author of dozens of songs and three musicals, Gavin has written lyrics with and for such luminaries as Sam Harris, Jake Heggie, Peter Allen, Chanticleer and Disney Studios. His classical art songs have been featured at Lincoln Center by mezzo Jennifer Larmore. He has written comedy with and for Dolly Parton, Joan Rivers, Peggy Lee, Vincent Price and Lily Tomlin. Two new musicals, *OMFG!!!* and *The Naked Poet* premiere in 2011 in San Francisco and Los Angeles, respectively.

❦

Eric Norris was born in Buffalo, New York, in 1968. He dabbled in astrophysics, archaeology, and classics as a student at Boston University, before he settled down to study English. His work appears in many online journals and e-zines as well the anthology, *This New Breed: Gents, Badboys & Barbarians*. Eric is the author of the epic poem *Takaaki* and a slender novella called *Terence*, a comic translation of A.E. Housman's *A Shropshire Lad*. Both are available on Lulu.com from Square Circle Press.

❦

About the Publisher

The mission of Sibling Rivalry Press is to develop, publish, and promote outlaw artistic talent—those projects which inspire people to read, challenge, and ponder the complexities of life in dark rooms, under blankets by cell-phone illumination, in the backseats of cars, and on spring-day park benches next to people reading Norse and Ginsberg. We welcome manuscripts which push boundaries, sing sweetly, or inspire us to perform karaoke in drag. Not much makes us flinch.

www.ingramcontent.com/pod-product-compliance
Lightning Source LLC
Chambersburg PA
CBHW021110090426
42738CB00006B/577